I AM
HEALING

ROSE GRANT

I AM
HEALING

Finding safety within

AUSTIN WYSE

with Jo Phillips

ROSE GRANT

First published 2013 by Rose Grant Publishing
Copyright © 2013 Rose Grant Publishing

ROSE GRANT

85 Killams Green, Taunton, Somerset TA1 3YQ, United Kingdom
Design | Sarah Anderson
Editor | Barbara Vesey

DISCLAIMER

The authors and publisher of this book are not licensed health professionals and do not dispense medical advice nor prescribe the use of any technique as a form of treatment for physical or medical problems without the advice of a licensed health professional, either directly or indirectly. The intent of the authors and publisher of this book is only to offer information of a general nature to help you in your search for good health and wellbeing. In the event that you use any of this information for yourself, the authors and publisher assume no responsibility.

A CIP catalogue record for this title is available from the British Library.

ISBN 978-0-9571533-2-5

Contents

Acknowlededgments

Jo and I would like to thank Barbara Vesey for her invaluable editing skills, Sarah Anderson for her cover design and Miles Bailey and his publishing team for their constant guidance and support.

There are many other people (mainly clients) whom I would like to thank for allowing me to share their experiences with them, but for obvious reasons I am unable to name them all specifically. Needless to say that these people gave me a deeper and richer understanding of the human condition and, indeed, of myself. Without their trust, honesty and openness this book would have been much more of a challenge to write.

Finally, I would also like to acknowledge all of the animal companions I have had over the years, from the rabbits, to the horses, to the cats. Our current cats, Nala and Newen, have watched over this book from start to finish. Their occasional scuffles, demands for food and constant requests for affection have served as welcome breaks to the frustrations of creating a book from scratch. There can be few things more satisfying than coming up with a much-needed word, metaphor or idea while watching a cat sleep or wash. This book is all the better for their presence.

Preface

The subject of healing is one I have been fascinated with for many years, because I believe healing (which means 'to become whole') is one of the most natural processes known to humanity, yet so many people find it unbelievably hard to connect with.

What Is Healing?

For me, healing is ultimately a phenomenon beyond comprehension. Yes, there are many experts who can explain different aspects of the process scientifically but, as with gravity or even electricity, when it comes to healing there is also an unknown element that no one can explain. For example, think of the last time you superficially cut your finger and miraculously over a few days the skin repaired itself. I'm sure you'll agree that no amount of understanding about the process or conscious wilful thought made that happen, and that is because healing takes place at a level below conscious awareness. In fact, if we were to stress about the cut, analyse the cut, ring up our friends and cry about the cut, the chances are we would inhibit the process somewhat, so this is why I firmly believe that healing occurs when we get all of our conscious and, crucially, *sub*conscious obstacles out of the way ... and just allow that unknown element to do its thing.

Just to be clear, I do fully recognise that even when we clear our conscious and subconscious obstacles there are still some physical or material conditions that cannot ever be perfectly restored back to full working order. For example, I once worked with a man whose arm was paralysed after a motorbike accident and he never got any amount of movement back in that limb, but he *was* able to heal the way he thought and felt about the accident and the events leading up to it. In fact, he actually told me on one occasion that losing the use of his arm was his single greatest life lesson because it had forced him to look at areas of his life that he hadn't been able to 'get a grip on'. Yes, he used those exact words. So although his arm didn't heal, healing did occur in his relationship with himself.

So you see, healing can be restorative (in the case of the cut finger) and it can also be transformative (in the case of the man who lost the use of his arm but gained inner peace). In other words, sometimes healing is completely invisible but other times it leaves physical scars. However, healing doesn't have to leave *emotional* scars that continue to weep, and that is the main focus of this book.

> *If you overreact to, or disengage with events in your life, you are very likely to have emotional scars that are continuing to weep. When people have healed their emotional scars they are able to go with the flow of life and be part of a transformative process.*

There may also be people who wonder how death fits into the healing process, because surely if we have this innate ability to heal, we would never die? This book is not about living forever, nor even about avoiding illness and disease. This book is about healing the way you think and feel about your unique challenges, so you can experience the fulfilment of your life and, ultimately, of your death.

> *'The fear of death follows from the fear of life. A man who lives fully is prepared to die at any time.'*
> – Mark Twain

A Deep Knowing

So, one of the main reasons I have been so fascinated with healing is because throughout my life I have met people who tell me about their injuries, their illnesses, their health conditions, their failed relationships, their empty bank accounts and their unhappy jobs and, despite feeling compassion for them, I would also have a deep knowing that these people didn't have to be suffering emotionally in the long-drawn-out way that they were.

When I talk about a 'deep knowing' I should explain that I am not talking about fortune-telling or an angel whispering in my ear. I am talking about my intuition (my inner teacher), which I believe is the ability that every single one of us has to recall wisdom from our cellular memories. In my case, my intuition is based on a lifetime of observing people, listening to stories and studying human consciousness. My intuition also comes from all the advanced technical problem-solving I did as an electronic engineer when I was a young man, and I believe it also comes from my mother.

As you will find out in the Introduction, my mother,

Carmal, was pretty terrible in lots of ways, but I can also acknowledge her gifts as well, and she was incredibly intuitive. I grew up watching her predict all sorts of situations, and actually I don't believe she was even aware she was doing it. She didn't practise as a psychic because, to her, this intuitive nature was 'the norm' – but can you imagine the impact her intuitive nature had on a little lad as his subconscious was being programmed? Thanks to my mother, intuition to me comes as naturally as eating a biscuit with a cup of tea (which is one of my favourite pastimes, by the way).

Even during conversations now, I will mention something seemingly random that comes into my mind to people and they will say to me, 'How did you know that?' Again, I don't say things to be flash and I, like my mother, don't identify myself with the psychic world. I feel that it is just a natural ability to access the memories that have been embedded in the cells of my mind and body, and because I am open and I have a strong sense of self I am able to get my ego out of the way and translate these memories into information that relates to the person I am with.

So you see, when I talk about a deep knowing that people don't have to be suffering emotionally in the way that they are suffering, it is a deep, profound knowing based on years of experience, observation and intuition, and one that I certainly cannot ignore. Yet so often when I make suggestions to people about ways they can begin to change their thoughts, their feelings and their behaviour so that they can begin to release themselves from their suffering, nothing happens. Or at least, if it does, it's very short-lived and, like a train returning to its well-worn tracks, the same old patterns come up time and again.

At first I considered the prospect that it must be something I was doing wrong, but I know that is just my ego talking, because I have made this journey myself and I know it is possible, plus I have worked with other people (like the motorbike rider) who are able to implement significant changes to their lives in the same way that a duck takes to water, so this was not a factor that needed to be considered. I also thought about the fact that suffering is a necessary part of life because it helps us grow and wakes us up to a new level of awareness, but then it occurred to me that it went deeper than that. I wanted to figure out why some people continue the lifespan of their suffering. Why are they stuck in their conscious and/or subconscious thoughts and feelings to a point where they find it difficult to move forward with their lives and heal?

We Long to Feel Safe

The answer I came up with, which I will go on to explain in much more detail throughout this book, is that remaining stuck in the same thoughts, feelings and behaviours allows people to feel safe.

> *Even if we have health conditions and our life is full of problems it can still make us feel safe, because we have an identity and we know who we are. You can read more about 'Secondary Gain' in my first book,* Without the Woo Woo, *but this book goes much more deeply into this kind of psychological reversal.*

If we let *new* thoughts, feelings and behaviours emerge, then our experiences change and we enter into the unknown. As you can imagine, though, when you have been wounded the idea of walking directly into the unknown is deeply unsettling and can make you feel incredibly insecure and unsafe, so like the Devil running from holy water you (subconsciously) do everything you can to avoid it.

> *It is important to recognise that there is an enormous difference between the feelings of not being certain and the feelings of not being safe. Uncertainty is a human need and helps us to grow and develop; we all need some uncertainty to keep us moving and motivated. However, we were never designed to feel unsafe unless our lives were in immediate danger. Prolonged feelings of being unsafe have a massive impact on our emotional and physical wellbeing, and keep us stuck.*

In this book I will outline some of the subconscious barriers that we can develop and maintain in an attempt to keep ourselves feeling safe. I believe that if we are able to collapse these barriers (through acknowledgment, reflection and self-development techniques), we stand a much better chance of accessing the 'unknown element' of healing and transforming our lives.

Introduction
Who Am I?

For as long as I can remember I have been fascinated by the human condition and what makes us do the things we do. I remember as a young boy growing up in Ireland making a conscious decision to listen intently to people when they came to our cottage to tell their stories. Inside my head, even as a little child I actually thought to myself, 'If I can understand *their* lives, I will be able to understand mine.'

I would also spend hours on my own, wandering around outside near our cottage in Kilkenny. One of my favourite things to do was to stand in the crystal-clear water of the stream and try and catch fish with my tiny bare hands after watching the patterns of their movements for hours on end. I also remember one day walking as far as I could, towards a mountain on the horizon, desperately wanting to know what was on the other side – only to find that, when I did make it to my longed-for vantage point, there was another mountain. However, even as a youngster of about six years old, my perception wasn't of endless obstacles; I felt exhilarated that another challenge lay before me, and this memory has become a metaphor that I teach and live by every day: there is always more to learn, more to discover.

Having said that, my childhood wasn't as idyllic as this may make it sound. My mother was a hopeless alcoholic, and another of my early memories is of her falling into a ditch full of stinging nettles after yet another drinking binge. I remember standing nearby crying because I was too small to pull her out. I grew up watching her drink herself senseless every day (until about the age of seven, when she put me into care). During the time that I lived with her I would pray for her to fall asleep most days, because I knew that when she woke up she would be OK for a while until the whole cycle started again.

The two-bedroom cottage was cramped with my grandparents, my mum, me and my older brother all living there, and our lives together were very basic. We grew our own vegetables, collected milk direct from the farm churns over the road, brought water back to the cottage from the well half a mile away, and even bathed in a tub by the fire. Looking back now I realise that my upbringing taught me so much about what is really important in life. It made me very grateful and humble.

The cottage in Kilkenny where I grew up, as it stands today.

However, one of the biggest emotions my early life lacked was love or affection of any kind. It was non-existent. In fact there was one Christmas when I remember wishing that my mum would cuddle us. I didn't want anything else, except to be held in her arms. Needless to say, that lack of affection continued, and when she was no longer able to care for us, she placed me and my brother in an orphanage in England. As far as love and affection were concerned, the nuns certainly took over where my mother had left off.

The derelict orphanage as it stood in the 1980s.

Far from the endless rolling views of green fields and mountains that I'd been used to in Ireland, I was now looking out at the streets of London from behind draughty sash windows in a Victorian dormitory filled with other boys. In the winter those windows would whistle and rattle in the cold wind, and on those nights, no matter how high I pulled my blanket up as I lay on the lumpy horsehair mattress, I would never get warm. I still joke today that those mattresses weren't just made of horsehair, they had the horses' hooves in them, too. They really were so uncomfortable.

I would always be hungry, too – never starving, but always hungry. Food was basic and we ate for survival, never for pleasure. I never felt full. In fact, I never felt abundance of any kind, I guess because nothing belonged to me. When my feet had got too big for my school shoes, I would be taken to the boot room and told to pick a pair of identical boots, just as ugly and just as 'used' as the pair I had grown out of. The only difference was they were a size bigger.

There were only two occasions when I felt special, but before I detail them it's worth saying that a year before I arrived at the orphanage the boys that lived there weren't even addressed by their names. They were given numbers. That really shows how impersonal and unloving this environment was, but thankfully, as I say, that practice had stopped before my arrival.

Ironically, the days I look back on with any kind of fondness were the days when I was in the infirmary, of all places! It is no surprise to me now that the emotional upheaval I was going through was taking its toll on my body, and as a result I was a very poorly child. However, despite my ill-health I don't have any bad memories of this time, being cared for by nurses, shovelling back regular meals, playing with jigsaw puzzles and watching *Tales of the Riverbank* in bed was as close to heaven as I ever felt back then.

Until, that is, I experienced the orphanage's Christmas parties, which were laid on by the American

Forces. There were sandwiches cut into triangles, cakes dripping with chocolate, fizzy drinks for burping competitions, and presents that well-meaning people had donated to kids like me who had known nothing of these treasures, and it was at one of these parties where I received a gift that would change the course of my life.

This gift was a crystal radio set that I adored. I would spend every moment I could listening to Radio Luxembourg, and when I wasn't listening I would be taking the thing apart to try and figure out how it worked. It was my pride and joy, and it was the first thing – and the only thing – that I ever really owned in the orphanage. So it is no surprise that, against all the odds, it inspired me to become an engineer. Not an easy thing to do when all the boys in the orphanage felt like they were at the bottom of the social pile, but I was determined (and still am now) not to be limited by the views of other people.

So at age 15, when I left the orphanage, I got myself a small room in Shepherd's Bush and did whatever I had to do to become that engineer. I had to keep finding out how things worked. The more things I took apart, the more things I wanted to take apart. The more things I fixed, the more things I wanted to fix. It was my dream career, until I realised that reason and logic aren't the answers to everything.

I have to point out here that, during this time, and because of my childhood experiences, I had not developed into a very nice person. I was angry, aggressive and unpredictable, and my unresolved emotions were holding me back. So in that room in Shepherd's Bush I remember one night looking in the mirror and realising that it was time for me to work out who I was and how *I* worked.

Up until now I had only tried to do this with other people, or pieces of equipment with no feelings. This challenge would be much harder and much more intimate, but I had no choice if I wanted to progress. So, alongside my work as an engineer for EMI, I started studying to become a counsellor and, over the years that followed, moved into different areas of complementary health care and 'energy medicine'. It is really interesting to me now that I never set out on my journey of self-discovery with the intention of helping other people; I wanted to understand me. However, the answers I found through my own experiences and through decades of study, observation and reflection were so universal I felt I had to share them.

So with those decades of experiences behind me, in 2012, alongside my colleague Dawn Bailey, I co-authored an entry-level self-development book called *Without the Woo Woo* with the aim of explaining complex concepts about mind, body and spiritual wellbeing without any technical or religious jargon. *Without the Woo Woo* had to be written to lay the foundations for this book.

In *I Am Healing* I want to take you deeper inside those understandings. I want to share with you the information I have gathered through my own experiences and years of study about why the human condition can sometimes find it difficult to heal. I want you to know what I have discovered about me so you don't just read the insights contained in *Without the Woo Woo*, you can actually live them and set yourself free.

I often ask myself why communicating information about the human condition is such a passion of mine. I guess it's the engineer in me. I would never stop until I understood a piece of equipment. And, of course, my ultimate aim was (as long as it still had potential) to get it working again.

So to answer the question in the title of this preamble, 'Who Am I?' I am an observer of life, always have been and always will be, and I am someone who wants to share my experiences and observations in the most simple way that I can to help other people.

> '*Any intelligent fool can make things bigger and more complex ... It takes a touch of genius – and a lot of courage – to move in the opposite direction.*'
> – Albert Einstein

With that quote from Einstein in mind, I would like to add that this book and *Without the Woo Woo* would not exist without my partner Jo Phillips, who somehow gathers all the words I speak into her head and practises them herself so she can translate them into the clear and concise words you are reading now. Jo is the spirit behind this book.

Principles to Keep in Mind

As you read through the pages of this book you may find it helpful to keep some of these basic principles in mind.

1. The Constructs of the Ego

Remember that this information may not always 'fit in' with the culture you have been brought up in. This is because so many cultures operate within the constructs of the ego. The ego has four main beliefs which are all centred on the idea of GETTING. More things. More status. More respect. More, more more. These beliefs are:

1. I am what I have.

2. I am what I do.

3. I am what other people think of me.

4. I am separate from everyone else.

The information in this book has one belief which is centred on the idea of GIVING:

1. I am what I am.

I would urge you to spend lots of time and energy in honest reflection about how many ego-constructs are deeply embedded in your subconscious. Bear in mind that they may be invisible at first glance, but they can be found when you do the inner work required. This inner work is so important because the ego can *never* make you feel safe, because it is externally focused and everything that isn't inside you is transient: it comes and goes. The foundations of this whole book are built on helping you develop a sense of internal security like never before, and you will find it very difficult to animate this if you are stuck in ego-consciousness.

> *It is only when we collapse the ego and its beliefs on an individual and a collective level that humanity will be able to live in harmony with Nature.*

2. Go Beyond Health

This book primarily focuses on empowering you to heal your physical and emotional wellbeing, but the information in the book can also be cross-referenced to other areas of your life. So if you are facing problems in your relationships, your finances, your career/vocation, read and re-read the chapters from a different headspace and consider how your subconscious barriers could be holding you up in every area of your life.

> *Let me be very clear: This information can potentially be cross-referenced to any problem you face. This is because the problem is very rarely the problem. The problem is usually your response to the problem. This book deals with changing your responses at a conscious and subconscious level.*

3. Your Healing Resides within You

Remember at all times that the healer resides in the individual who is doing the healing in their own mind, body and spirit. In no way, shape or form am I suggesting that I am a healer, only in the sense that I take responsibility for my own healing in my own life. The words 'I Am' which I have chosen for the powerful title of this book are to be used in the context of yourself, as the final chapter will explain in more detail.

'Healing is a state of being.' – Eric Pearl

4. Don't Be in a Rush to 'Fix' Everything

Much of the information in this book will create new thoughts, new neurological pathways for you, especially because it is written in such a clear, concise and relatable way. However, that doesn't mean you will instantly have all the tools to correct the issues that need correcting. Throughout this book I will constantly be reminding you to sit with your new understandings, absorb them and analyse them in the context of your own unique experiences. The information in this book took me years (maybe even decades) to observe and experience in myself, and there are still aspects I continue to open up to. This book is about helping you understand who you are at a profoundly deep level, and often the best way to access that information is in stillness and silence. I do understand that this can be difficult for many people, so I have created various recordings to help you with the process of stopping distractions and going inside for answers, which you may find extremely beneficial (see my website www.thewysecentre.co.uk). Meanwhile, having made that point about meditation and relaxation, I am not suggesting you put your life on pause and cease living, I am just asking that you refrain from asking the questions 'What do I do now?' or 'How do I get rid of this?' until you have gathered all the necessary information about yourself in your peaceful, yet highly productive reflections.

> *Don't make a decision or a choice until you have all the information.*

5. Go Back to Basics

Make sure you have a copy of my first book *Without the Woo Woo* close by. *Without the Woo Woo* lays the foundations for the more in-depth information you will read in this book, and you will find it useful for reference. Just like *Without the Woo Woo*, this book will change as you change, and as time passes you will read it for the third time and understand some things you didn't when you read it for the first and second time. This is because when you gain a new conscious understanding from reading words, you will attract a new experience into your life which then embeds the meaning of the words and the subsequent experience you had into your subconscious.

> *Only when something is absorbed at a subconscious level can it be fully utilised.*

6. This Is Not the End

This book is not and could never hope to be the definitive book on finding out who you are and why you do what you do, but it will give you the head-start that I wish I'd had when I began looking at myself in the mirror. I also believe that the more you investigate this book, along with different aspects of spirituality, complementary health and even the non-profit-driven side of conventional medicine, you will notice commonly occurring themes that all seem to add up and make sense for you.

> *'The truth is incontrovertible. Malice may attack it, ignorance may deride it, but in the end, there it is.'*
> – **Winston Churchill**

Chapter 1
I Am No Longer the Babe

'Study the past if you would define the future.'
– Confucius

I doubt many people spend much effort thinking about or reflecting on their time in the womb and their subsequent first few months of life, but I firmly believe that if we want to begin to heal any aspect of our lives, this is a wonderfully fascinating area to explore, because this is where we begin to form our emotional subconscious perceptions about how safe the world is and how safe we feel within it.

One of the golden rules about any aspect of self-development or personal growth is that security and safety are not to be found in the external world; they are inner experiences that must be cultivated. When you feel safe and secure, both consciously and subconsciously, you are more receptive and open to healing so that transformation can take place.

So in order to get in touch with your early life experiences and obtain wisdom about your own inner security, let's consider an ideal environment for a baby to develop a sense of safety from conception through to birth. Please note that I am not expressing any personal views or opinions here; this example is purely to help you build a picture of how a subconscious feeling of inner security might develop *in utero*. I would also ask that you refrain from reading this chapter from the perspective of a parent; rather, you read it with the desire to find out more about yourself first. After all, we can only teach our children what we ourselves learn.

The Safety of the Womb

First of all, then, in an 'ideal world' the baby is conceived in love, purposefully between two adults. So even from the moment the sperm fertilises the egg, the foetus feels a sense of belonging and acceptance at a very deep level. As the foetus begins to grow he is surrounded by cushioning and protection. He is in constant connection with the reassuring resonance of his mother's steady heartbeat, attuned to her muffled calming voice and life-affirming breath. He is given automatic sustenance and is enveloped in his mother's emotional state of equilibrium, harmony and balance. He is suspended in a place where Nature is taking care of everything, effortlessly. He doesn't have to 'work hard' to grow his legs, his arms or even his nose; his role is to simply 'be' and surrender in the comforting warmth and loving security of his mother's belly.

After the full nine months, when the baby sends the signals to mum that he is ready, the pair then experience a natural delivery without medical intervention. Mum relies on the innate wisdom of her mind, body and spirit to guide her baby out into the world while he completes his own hugely important and empowering birthing process. He is then placed on his mother's naked breast to feed while life-long bonds are forged through eye contact, thoughts, words, skin (the biggest organ of the body) and emotions. As a result of this entire process it would be easy to conclude that this baby would feel safe, secure and unconditionally loved.

> *Inner security and safety aren't just part of some intellectual theory; they are physical feelings that resonate inside and outside of our entire being, allowing us to be fully present in any situation.*

Can you imagine how safe you would feel in your life now if you had experienced this 'ideal world' scenario? Perhaps your experience came pretty close, or perhaps you can't relate at all. At this moment in time it isn't necessary to have all the answers, I just want you to absorb the concept and make a connection between how safe you feel now and how safe you may have felt from the moment of your own conception, right through to your arrival into the world.

What If You Didn't Have the 'Ideal World' Experience?

There may be people reading this now who still feel that I am making judgements about babies who didn't experience the 'ideal world' scenario that I have just described, but nothing could be further from the truth. We seem to be living in a farcical world of political correctness where we can't express Nature's 'ideal' for fear of making people feel bad if they didn't achieve it. This is total nonsense. This isn't about going back and changing what happened to make it 'perfect', because what is done is done. This isn't about right or wrong, good or bad, failure or success. This is about the *reality* of finding out what emotional tools we weren't given, so we can eventually give those emotional tools to ourselves. This is about personal responsibility. Nothing more, nothing less.

My intention in this chapter is to offer information to help you begin to acknowledge how feelings of security and safety from conception to birth and beyond have the potential to influence us subconsciously for the rest of our lives. Many people prefer to believe that their conception, time *in utero* and birth are now completely irrelevant and, even if they weren't, there is nothing they can do about it now, but this is most certainly not the case. Every single thing that happened to you during your incarnation into this world helped to form the person you are and the way you respond today, and it is my own belief and my own experience that if those responses are now redundant, with awareness and an open mind and heart they can be changed.

> *Don't let anyone tell you that the start you had in life doesn't have the potential to have an impact on your feelings today, because it does.*

Even new-thinking scientists now accept that your subconscious programming begins in the womb and the subconscious is where you function from 97 per cent of the time.

There But for the Grace of God Go I

I think it is also worth saying that I am very aware that there are people who may be reading this and wondering how all of this knowledge relates to babies who are born with serious abnormalities, health conditions or even terminal illnesses. You may even be trying to make sense of miscarriages or stillbirths, or any number of other so-called 'wrong-doings' when it comes to creating a new life. My answer to this is that there is so much of life we don't understand or could ever even hope to understand, and I am sharing my observations with an enormous amount of humility about the unknown and also from the perspective of someone who has experienced infant death in his own family. I'm not trying to glibly explain illness and disease, or why things happen as they do, because there are millions of different factors for every individual on the planet.

I am, however, suggesting that if you want to become someone who is more open and receptive to healing an area of your life, then developing a deeper sense of inner security and safety (whatever your state of mind, body or spirit) is a fundamental part of that healing, both on an individual and collective level. In order to do this in the most powerful way possible, understanding your subconscious programming needs to be part of the equation and (as new science is now recognising) our subconscious programming begins in the womb.

For more information on the subconscious, please refer to Insight 4 'Your Subconscious is Powerful' in Without the Woo Woo

Also bear in mind that the process of personal growth isn't about getting instant answers that have been scientifically proven and labelled; it is about making a long-term commitment to discovering who you really are, which will ultimately allow you to function at a higher level of consciousness. This is a process that requires you to use and refine your own inner guidance system, which can only be engaged when your desire for truth becomes insatiable. On your journey you will come up against questions that have no answers, but even acknowledging the fact that you 'don't know' something or that something is missing can be enormously empowering. Again, try not to focus on wrong or right, good or bad, success or failure … and just place your attention on the reality so that you can move forward.

> *'Grant me the serenity to accept the things I cannot change; courage to change the things I can; and wisdom to know the difference.'* – **Reinhold Niebuhr**

Feeling Safe in the External World

So now let's return to the example of the baby who has just been born after nine months of bliss in the sanctuary of his mother's womb. You'd be right to think that even the baby who had experienced deep feelings of security and safety from the moment of conception to the moment of birth would still be feeling slightly overwhelmed by his new surroundings. Think about it: within a few moments every one of his five senses is instantly heightened and his life changes from an internal reality to an external one. He suddenly has to navigate a completely different environment, and that is why he arrives fully equipped with a set of safety mechanisms called 'primitive reflexes'.

What Are Primitive Reflexes?

Primitive reflexes can be described as automatic, immediate movements that are executed without any conscious control. They develop *in utero* and their purpose is to keep the baby safe during the first few hazardous months of life. In an 'ideal world' these primitive reflexes are inhibited by higher centres of the brain during different stages of childhood development.

However, it is my belief and experience that if we don't develop the appropriate feelings of inner security and safety at the appropriate times, if we don't feel that the world is a safe place, it is possible for us to retain or even reactivate aspects of our primitive reflexes in an attempt to look after ourselves subconsciously. Before we explore this further, though, let's look at just one primitive reflex in more detail to give you an idea of the significant role that these reflexes play.

The Moro Reflex

The Moro reflex is an involuntary reaction to threat and was first discovered and described by Austrian paediatrician Ernst Moro, who believed that it is essentially a grasping reflex that helps an infant cling to his mother while she carries him around all day. If the infant loses his grip, the reflex causes the infant to embrace his mother and regain his hold on his mother's body.

The Moro reflex can be triggered if the infant feels as if he is falling, if there is a sudden unexpected occurrence of any kind, if he is in pain or if he is being handled too roughly. Other factors like temperature change or even a change in head position can also trigger the Moro reflex.

When triggered, the Moro reflex causes the baby to open his arms and legs and then close his arms and legs as if to embrace or clasp, but these movements are not the only responses taking place. The infant will also simultaneously experience rapid breathing, a triggering of the immune system which activates the fight, flight or freeze response, increased heart rate, raised blood pressure, reddening of the skin and a possible outburst of anger or tears, all in just a few moments.

> *The role of the Moro reflex is to alert, arouse and to summon assistance. It is also thought to play a major part in helping the baby to breathe in utero and also helps to open the windpipe if there is a threat of suffocation.*

The Effects of Retaining or Reactivating the Moro Reflex

The Moro reflex emerges just nine weeks after conception so is fully present at birth and, all things being well, it is inhibited between the first two and four months of life and is then transformed into the adult 'startle response'. However, if all or even just residual elements of the Moro reflex are retained or reactivated after this time, there can be many profound effects.

> *The reason why the effects of retaining or reactivating primitive reflexes are so profound is because they are supposed to have a limited lifespan; they exist to help the baby survive the first few hazardous months of life so that the baby feels confident, safe and secure about learning life skills.*

Some of the effects of retaining or reactivating the Moro reflex include poor balance and coordination, visual perception problems, motion sickness, fatigue, auditory confusion, poor immune function, anxiety seemingly unrelated to reality, muscle tension, mood swings and even a need to control or manipulate events. Fascinatingly, the Moro reflex is the only one of the primitive reflexes to be connected in some way to all of the senses, so is it any wonder that the effects of retaining or reactivating it after its natural lifespan are so far-ranging?

Look again at all the responses that take place when the Moro reflex is activated: rapid breathing, activation of fight, flight or freeze, anger and tears, etc. It stands to reason that if this reflex isn't inhibited at the end of its natural lifespan, then these automatic responses continue in the individual until such time as new life skills are learned.

I'm hoping that even this brief insight into just one reflex is now giving you a deeper understanding of human behaviour. Yes, exercise, diet, supplements, medications, surgeries, organic cosmetics and products all have their place and can alleviate and even remove some of the symptoms, but until we start to instil a sense of safety and security in disrupted individuals by addressing redundant conscious and subconscious behaviour, we are barely scratching the surface.

Why Might the Reflex Have Been Retained?

Lots of experts have suggested reasons why the Moro reflex is retained, and these include birth trauma, lack of movement as a result of being placed for long periods of time in car seats or in front of television sets, injuries, reactions to environmental toxins and disruptions in the family. While all of these are helpful indicators, it is very plain for me to conclude that, once again, it all comes down to how safe and secure the baby feels at a very deep level. If for whatever reason we lose a conscious sense of our own personal safety and security, it stands to reason that our all-knowing subconscious will offer the solution of a primitive reflex which will give us that subconscious feeling of security we so desperately crave – albeit an outdated one.

Why Might a Reflex Be Reactivated?

I believe the same conclusion can be reached for an individual who reactivates aspects of a primitive reflex. At a deep level they don't feel safe, so in the absence of a learned life skill their all-knowing subconscious reactivates a solution that worked in the past.

All Our Problems Were Once Solutions

However, when this 'solution' happens, problems ensue later, because now the individual who subconsciously uses the Moro reflex is experiencing the *effects* of retaining or activating it. So all the anxiety, triggering of the immune system, fatigue, need to control and manipulate become anchored to an outdated feeling of safety. This to me is such an obvious reason why people hold on to negative behaviour patterns, because if a primitive reflex is still active past its natural lifespan, they associate its effects with a redundant sense of safety.

One of the ways we naturally develop a meaningful sense of safety is by fully experiencing life in the external world, because this allows us to learn and grow, even when we make mistakes. However, the individual who retains or reactivates a primitive reflex becomes very internally focused and subconsciously fearful of new situations that might trigger the reflex and its effects. As a result they avoid experiencing life, which means they aren't able to develop a sense of safety through learning, growing and making mistakes. So, as bizarre as it might sound, they actually subconsciously sabotage doing the very things that *would* give them that meaningful feeling of security.

How Do You Heal Primitive Reflexes?

The main aim of this book is to give you information for you to acknowledge at a deep level and spend lots of time researching in the context of your own unique experiences. Once again, there is no magic pill or quick fix when it comes to primitive reflexes, but the first step to healing anything is always wisdom and knowledge. You may also be thinking after reading about primitive reflexes that instilling a sense of safety is of paramount importance, and you'd be right, but even this has to be done with love, patience and an enormous amount of expertise. Think about it: if you suddenly take away a safety mechanism that someone has been using for decades and glibly tell them to start using another one, you will make them feel even more insecure and could make matters worse. No, healing primitive reflexes is a specialised area, but that doesn't stop you becoming informed about them.

Having said that, I will be detailing some ideas later in this book to help you develop your healing potential in general; these behaviours would be wonderful to adopt alongside any relevant programme you choose to help you release primitive reflexes that may still be active.

There are many more primitive reflexes for you to research in your own time and your own way, but hopefully the information I have given you about the Moro reflex will whet your appetite for discovering the core issues of why we sometimes behave the way we behave. As I said earlier, yes, exercise, diet, supplements, medications, surgeries, organic cosmetics and products can all help us heal and stay healthy, but unless we address the underlying causes of our unrest, we are barely scratching the surface. For me the cause always comes back to how safe we feel and how our subconscious mind and body respond to our feelings of insecurity.

> *Once again it is important to recognise that there is
> an enormous difference between the feelings of not
> being certain and the feelings of not being safe.
> Uncertainty is a human need and helps us to grow
> and develop; we all need some uncertainty to keep us
> moving and motivated. However, we were never
> designed to feel unsafe unless our lives were in
> immediate danger. Prolonged feelings of being unsafe
> have a massive impact on our emotional and physical
> wellbeing, and keep us stuck.*

Misinterpretation and Insecurity

Moving on from primitive reflexes, you may also be interested in some information about how some aspects of your five senses – taste, touch, smell, hearing and sight – may have been subconsciously programmed when you were a baby. Although I won't be addressing all of the five senses in detail, I want to expand on how we can learn to misinterpret visual and auditory cues if we grew up around feelings of insecurity.

So let's return to our baby in the 'ideal world' who has now been breastfed by Mum for several months. It makes total sense to me, after studying the work of Dr Steven Porges, that while they have been looking adoringly into each other's eyes during feeding times, this tiny human form is constantly monitoring the subtle tone of his mum's facial muscles. If her facial muscle tone indicates tightness or stress, this is the subconscious programme the baby learns. If her facial muscles are calm or relaxed, this is the programme that becomes embedded. This means that we actually learn to read the subtleties of other people's facial expressions from what we see in our mum's facial muscle tone during our formative years, which is wonderful if your mum was a congruent human being. However, many of us would have been given a certain amount of corrupt information, so as we grow older and we begin to interact with other people, there is every chance that we continue to misread and misinterpret these subtle facial expressions. This is important because when we misread and misinterpret we create barriers to communication, and that causes disruption in our minds and bodies, meaning that once again at a level below conscious awareness we don't feel safe.

It is important to recognise that I am talking about the baby monitoring tiny, minute, subtle, minuscule, almost implicit, even energetic changes in Mum's facial muscle tone that would most probably go unnoticed by anyone else. It is also important to say that although I am constantly referencing Mum, this information is applicable to Dad as well, or indeed anyone who is part of the baby's bonding process during these formative years. Obviously Mum would have the most powerful influence in this subconscious programming because of the closeness involved in the pregnancy and birthing process, but in the absence of Mum, the baby will look for other references.

How We Interpret Sounds as Babies

Another way we learn to feel safe is through our ability to hear. It makes total sense to most people that if we are unable to hear effectively we are more likely to feel vulnerable. You only have to watch a cat outside on a windy day to understand this reality. Cats hate the wind because it interferes with their highly tuned hearing mechanisms, meaning they are less able to identify approaching danger and feel unsafe. It is the same for us: the ability to hear helps us to feel safe.

Of course some people are born with or even develop varying degrees of medical deafness, but I don't just want you to focus on that, I want you to become aware of the fact that we all have the ability to *interpret* sounds incorrectly as well, without being medically diagnosed with a hearing problem.

As an example of this let's return to our baby in the 'ideal world' again. Can you imagine how he might interpret the sound of a loud house alarm if he is snuggled close to his calm and comforting mother while she finds the codes to turn the noisy interruption off? All the time she is reassuring him that there is nothing to worry about and even allows him to release his shock after the ringing has subsided by stroking and touching his body while he returns to equilibrium. That's right, the chances are that this baby would have interpreted this sound in a healthy way, he would have felt shock at a loud noise, which is absolutely natural, but he will also have subconsciously learned to keep situations like this in perspective.

However, as we have already discovered not everyone is exposed to this learning in the ideal world and may experience adults panicking at house alarms and other loud noises, so that when they grow up they may interpret some sounds in an unhealthy way.

Can you imagine what a frightening place the world might be for someone who hasn't learned to interpret sounds correctly? This is why whenever people tell me they suffer with panic attacks or anxiety, I will always ask questions about their hearing and their early experiences of interpreting sounds. We were given our five senses to help us feel safe in the world, so if one or more is not functioning or interpreting the environment correctly for whatever reason, it stands to reason that we won't feel safe.

The Developing Brain

The final aspect I would like to touch on in this chapter about our subconscious childhood development is the brain. Obviously the subject of the brain is huge and can be made very complex, but there are a few pieces of relevant information I would like to share with you from my own study about the brain that are simple and empowering and may help you on your quest of self-discovery.

First, you may have heard it said by conventional thinkers that we use only a small percentage of our brain. To me this seems utterly ridiculous. I do believe that there are parts of the brain that we don't yet understand, but that doesn't mean we don't use them or don't have the ability to use them. It is also worth noting our brains keep changing as we change. Modern research has demon-strated that the brain continues to create new neurological pathways and alter existing ones in order to adapt to new experiences, learn new information and create new memories.

Secondly, there is a part of the brain that actually relates to affiliation, which is a person's need to feel a sense of involvement and 'belonging' within a social group. Now I believe that this part of the brain is hugely significant when it comes to finding out who we are at a deep level. This is because very often the first obstacle that we meet when we begin to make changes in our lives is our anxiety about what people will think, especially the people we are affiliated with. This part of the brain can be very significant for some people who have been programmed with 'tribal' beliefs since birth. In fact, I have met people on several occasions who would rather have died, and in some cases have died, rather than let go of their affiliations. What is interesting to me, though, is that the mere act of becoming conscious of this area of the brain is very often enough to lessen (and even release) its hold for some people.

Finally, my personal research and study also led me to investigate the prefrontal cortex, which is a region of the brain that deals with reason and logic, or what is sometimes referred to in psychology as 'executive function'.

Executive function relates to abilities to differentiate among conflicting thoughts, determine good and bad, better and best, same and different, future consequences of current activities, working towards a defined goal, prediction of outcomes, expectation based on actions, and social 'control' (the ability to suppress urges that, if not suppressed, could lead to socially unacceptable outcomes).

Modern research is now discovering that people who were brought up in environments where they didn't feel emotionally or physically safe have prefrontal cortexes that are underdeveloped.

> *In the case of the prefrontal cortex, the term 'underdeveloped' doesn't mean big or small. It relates to the density of that region of the brain.*

This helped me to determine that when our prefrontal cortex is underdeveloped we are not able to use our executive function effectively, and when this happens we remain in situations where we feel very unsafe.

Once again I must stress that modern research is now showing that the brain is plastic, so I believe it is possible for us to help ourselves to develop our prefrontal cortexes. So much so that I have actually devised a simple tapping technique, which I will detail in the 'Five I Am Healing Behaviours' chapter later in this book. I am not claiming that the tapping technique increases the density of the prefrontal cortex, but my experience is that it is wonderfully relaxing and, when we feel relaxed, we feel safe.

In conclusion, I should point out that there is so much more information I could have included in this chapter to explain how significant our early subconscious programming is, but I am very aware that some of my observations may already be overwhelming. If that is the case, please just take the time to read the chapter again and again until it begins to make more sense, and always read it from the mindset that you have the potential to access the healing that you need when you feel a deep sense of safety.

Chapter 2
I Am the Languages I Use

'At the end of the day people won't remember what you said or did, they will remember how you made them feel.' – Maya Angelou

How would you feel if I opened this chapter by telling you that language is inseparable from healing? Yes, the languages you were exposed to and how you perceived those languages during your formative years are inextricably linked to your physical and emotional wellbeing today.

This chapter is so important to understand because our language originates from the subconscious and determines how we express ourselves. If we are unable to express ourselves effectively, we don't feel safe, and if we don't feel safe, we are constantly (and needlessly) triggering our immune system, living in chaos and inhibiting the healing process.

Explicit and Implicit Language

Let me explain, because when you think about language you probably think about words spoken in English, French, German or indeed any other dialect from different countries around the world. But language is so much more than words, because, crucially, language involves feelings as well.

A good way to understand this concept is to think of explicit language and implicit language. Explicit language is where the words are clearly stated in detail and leave no room for doubt or confusion. Implicit language is where the interactions are implied and understood through feelings, and not directly expressed. The way we communicate with ourselves and others is a mix of both, because where you have human beings interacting, you will always have words and feelings.

It Isn't What We Say, It's How We Say It

For example, imagine saying 'Good morning' to someone in the street and feeling a sense of happiness and light on every level as you greet that stranger. Now imagine saying 'Good morning' to that same person on the same street, but deep down inside you feel a sense of stress and anxiety instead. You get a totally different feeling in your mind and body, don't you? And, guess what? – on some very subtle energetic level, so does the stranger. At a level below conscious awareness, the stranger not only picks up on your explicit language (words) but your implicit language (feelings) as well, and in turn acts accordingly to the languages they themselves have learned.

How You Learned Your Languages

As I explained in *Without the Woo Woo*, during our formative years between the ages of birth and six, our brains are not fully developed and are functioning at levels below consciousness. We are operating at a brain frequency known as *theta*, so our experiences feel almost 'dreamlike', 'hypnotic' and 'meditative'. As a result the words and feelings we are exposed to (along with lots of other information) become embedded into our subconscious as automatic responses.

New science is now revealing that we operate from our subconscious 97 per cent of the time, so what we learn during our formative years is fundamental to our physical and emotional wellbeing in later life.

The Power of Love and Intimacy

Now this process is already pretty powerful, but it actually gets more intense when we realise the significance of the people who taught us our explicit and implicit languages. Our mother and father figures and/or primary care-givers had authority over us and we depended on them for survival. They would also have been teaching us these languages through the perceptions of love and intimacy which are key drivers of the human condition from birth to death, so everything they said and everything they felt would have had an enormous hold over what our subconscious absorbed.

Be in no doubt, the words and feelings from 'authority' figures whom you were depending on for survival, love and intimacy during your formative years would have been embedded into your

> *subconscious. Unless the explicit and implicit*
> *languages that are no longer serving you have been*
> *addressed, the chances are that you are still using*
> *those words and feelings to some degree today.*

Now, whenever I share this information, almost without exception people start to feel blame or guilt. So it is important to point out that the people around you who taught you these languages were doing the best they could with the skills they had, and that sentiment is the same if you yourself are now teaching languages to a child. The important thing always to recognise is that the past is the past. We must learn from it and take responsibility for what we can do today to change for the better.

> *Guilt is a luxury we can no longer afford.*
> *Blame is unproductive and keeps you stuck in the*
> *past.*

What Matters Most, Words or Feelings?

In my opinion it is without doubt that our feelings are where we live. Think about the 'Good morning' example. The words in both instances are the same, but the feelings are quite different, and feelings, like it or not, are oftentimes much more powerful than words. The quote that opens this chapter illustrates this point very clearly.

Another reason why implicit languages are so powerful is because feelings (by their very nature) create an energetic charge in our conscious and subconscious minds and bodies that is remembered far, far, far longer than a thought or a word. Again, to give you a reference point for this, can you remember what your favourite teacher said to you during your first term at school? The answer is probably no, but you will certainly remember how they made you feel during your first term at school.

Having said all of that, we must never lose sight of the power that words have. Words, as we know, can do a great amount of damage – but they can also do a great amount to heal. I'm sure everyone can think of a time in their life where they have felt hopeless and at their wits' end, only to be given a powerful verbal insight about how they can get back on track. Explicit language has the ability to give someone a new neurological pathway in their brain, which can in turn change the biochemistry in the body and change their interactions, not only with themselves but with others as well. So be in no doubt that words are indeed very powerful tools for transformation, especially when they are combined congruently with feelings.

My Story – The Power of Words

As a young boy in the orphanage I remember being intentionally heavy-handed with one of my playmates. I hadn't been taught the implicit languages of gentleness and kindness from my mother, of course, but there was still no excuse for hurting someone else on purpose, and deep down I knew it. My feelings were confirmed when one of the teachers, rather than giving me a clip round the ear (as was

continued

the norm back then) actually took me to one side and explicitly said to me, 'How would you feel if someone did that to you?' I think being the damaged child that I was at the time I replied 'I wouldn't care,' but because the teacher didn't argue back with me I was forced inside my own thoughts to contemplate my actions, and that lesson is one I remember to this very day. Every time I interact with anyone now, I remember the words that teacher said to me, which are deeply embedded in my subconscious. 'How would you feel if someone did that to you?' Hopefully this illustrates the healing power of words, because in this example, the teacher didn't just heal me; he helped me to have empathy for others so I didn't intentionally hurt anyone else. I must point out here that I'm sure there are people reading this who will have been hurt by me through the process of life, but after that event in my life it is never something I would ever have intentionally set out to do. Sometimes it is necessary to use the same languages as other people to protect what you know is the truth, but that is another insight for another book.

Focus On Feelings

So explicit language is important, but it still cannot be stressed strongly enough that feelings speak louder than words, which is why it can be quite amusing to hear some parents say that they are 'careful' about using certain words around their children like 'hate' or 'ugly' or even 'no.' However, those same parents have been known to have feelings of hate, or feelings of being ugly or feelings of saying 'no', but instead of expressing their thoughts, words and feelings congruently, they suppress and teach nothing but confusion.

> *When children are brought up in environments that focus mainly on explicit language, they grow up feeling insecure because they have no idea how to interpret feelings, and our feelings are where we live.*

In some cases there are children who are never taught how to feel or process appropriately feelings like anger, sadness, grief, etc., so as a result they become adults who are unable to feel and use these necessary human emotions. I have lost count of the amount of people I have met who are crippled by physical pain because they were never taught how to feel and process their feelings with clarity.

> *'What the mind suppresses the body expresses.'*
> – Chinese proverb

Languages that Resonate

So the feelings that we learn in childhood (whether learned in confusion or clarity) become our implicit languages that we use throughout life and, just like speaking an explicit language like French or English, we can only really understand other people and be understood by other people who resonate with the same implicit languages as us, because if we haven't experienced a feeling ourselves, how can we ever begin to interpret it?

We learn implicit languages and then attract people into our lives who match or reflect those feelings which our whole being has become attuned to.

For example, if you felt humiliation at the hands of the people who were teaching you love and intimacy when you were growing up, even if you had no idea what the word 'humiliation' meant, you will have stored those feelings in your subconscious as part of your language, and you will continue to interact with yourself and with others at a subconscious level using that language of humiliation until such time as you address it.

It is important to point out that, just as you can learn a new explicit language, you can also learn new implicit languages. There is nothing you have learned that can't be unlearned with awareness and commitment. It also goes without saying that we can learn beneficial implicit languages such as trust, security, empowerment, etc., but the focus of this book is understanding the parts of ourselves that need to be addressed so that we can individually and collectively heal.

You may be thinking, 'This is silly, why would I continue using an implicit language that is negative and that is no longer serving me?' The answer is that your languages are deeply embedded in your subconscious. As I explained earlier, your subconscious was initially programmed at a time when your brain was operating at a frequency known as *theta*, between the ages of birth and six. A *theta* brainwave feels meditative, dreamlike and hypnotic, so when these languages were being embedded you didn't have the luxury of reason and logic to tell you they were unacceptable, which is why now they are triggered automatically (and sometimes even invisibly to you) when someone or something pushes your 'hot button'.

My Story – My Implicit Languages

As I have already explained, I grew up with an alcoholic mother for the first seven years of my life, in an environment that was void of any love and affection, both explicitly and implicitly. Those early experiences of heartache were compounded when I was placed in an orphanage with nuns who would swap jobs within the home at regular intervals so none of the boys became attached to any one of the Sisters. I learned many unhealthy implicit languages during my childhood including 'rejection' and 'abandonment', and it took me several professional and personal relationships to realise how my early programming had affected me. I attracted people into my life who understood the languages of 'rejection' and 'abandonment' as well, and we continued to reject and abandon each other until such time as the penny dropped and I was able to heal the feelings within. Now 'rejection' and 'abandonment' are no longer part of my implicit language in an unhealthy way, and I am actually grateful that I was able to experience and release these feelings because it helps me to empathise with other people in a very powerful and constructive way.

Examples of Implicit Languages

Here are some examples of implicit languages I have observed people using that have a negative effect on every area of their life. Sometimes I see people using these languages with all the best intentions, but I still understand how unnecessary they are.

Control · Fear · Rejection · Selfishness · Obsession · Greed · Aggression · Blame · Humiliation · Deceitfulness · Self-pity · Anger · Resentment · Bitterness · Negativity · Powerlessness · Attention-seeking · Entitlement · Inferiority · Superiority · Chaos · Playing dumb · Confusion · Guilt · Punishment · Torture · Childishness

This list is not exhaustive, but may help you think more deeply about the implicit languages that you have which may not be serving you anymore. However, it never fails to amaze me how invisible these behaviours can be to the person themselves, but I never judge because I understand how very often these subconscious languages have become protection mechanisms and are not representative of the 'real' person. However, the benefits of recognising and releasing them are immense, and the process of letting them go opens up exciting doors on the journey of self-discovery.

How Can I Identify My Implicit Languages?

It is well known that people find it exceptionally hard to identify their own behaviour patterns, and determining your own implicit languages is no exception. However, with a desire to become aware, anything is possible.

One of the best places to begin to identify your own implicit languages is to study discreetly and dispassionately the implicit languages your parents or primary care-givers use or used. Just bear in mind, though, that these implicit languages would have been open to your own interpretations. Think of the brother and sister who grow up in the same house with the same parents but who have a different interpretation of the implicit languages they were exposed to. With this in mind it may be interesting to consider that we are capable not only of copying the exact implicit language but also reflecting or reversing that implicit language. For example, if your mother-figure implicitly used the language of denial, you may grow up to use that language of denial in the very same way, or you may be someone who grows up learning acceptance which could be one of the reflections or reversals of denial.

It may also be that you are unable to study your primary care-givers' implicit languages because they are no longer alive, or you are no longer in touch with them, but that doesn't stop you remembering past interactions, watching old home videos or asking other people who knew them for more information.

> *It is so important to remember that when you begin*
> *to ask questions about why you are who you are and*
> *why you feel the way you feel that you may never get*
> *the precise, correct, exact answers you are looking*
> *for, but you will get information and even if you*
> *don't know what that information is telling you, it*
> *will broaden your mind and it will allow you to*
> *connect with yourself in a deeper and more*
> *meaningful way.*

In fact, asking yourself unanswerable questions is a wonderful way to access the wisdom of the subconscious, because it allows us to get reason and logic out the way. Another fascinating and somewhat mind-boggling idea to consider is how new science is revealing that we may also learn implicit languages in the womb. The developing baby is not only sharing a body with Mum, he is also sharing her mind and her spirit which, as we know, are inseparable anyway. Together this body/mind/spirit from Mum communicates her feelings to her unborn baby so he can have some awareness of the external environment he is entering into. Again, for someone who never knew their biological mother, this may make identifying your own implicit languages during this stage harder, but if you are aware of it you can still contemplate, imagine and reflect on what feelings you may have been exposed to while you were *in utero*.

> 'When you touch one thing with deep awareness, you
> touch everything.' – **Thich Nhat Hanh**

As well as researching your formative years, you can also start to identify your own implicit languages by asking people who are close to you for their perceptions of the feelings you are using during everyday communication. When doing this it is important to make sure you ask people you trust, and also to bear in mind that these people may well have their own perceptions and misperceptions, but if you ask a few individuals you may start to notice similar answers or patterns which will allow you to address the implicit languages that are no longer serving you by bringing the new realisations to your conscious awareness.

> *There are lots of new ideas and ancient techniques to re-programme the subconscious, but we can often change the subconscious in beneficial ways just by bringing a much-needed realisation to our conscious awareness.*

Your Languages Have an Impact on Every Area of Your Life

The implicit languages that you use are not just influential in the relationships you have, they are inextricably linked to your entire physical existence. The way you feel about money, the way you feel about your job or career, even the way you feel about your state of health or disease are all connected to the implicit languages you were exposed to in childhood and how you interpreted them. However, before you start shouting this discovery from the rooftops, take heed that uncovering and addressing these aspects of yourself is not something that anyone enters into lightly.

Not an Easy Task

So much so that Teresa of Avila, a sixteenth-century Spanish saint, called these negative implicit languages 'reptiles', which builds a really powerful picture of what happens to you when they surface. She believed that it was impossible to find your soul if you had reptiles inside you.

Interestingly, the subject of 'reptiles' is not one that is often covered in the mind/body/spirit realm because it is much easier to talk about medications, supplements, spa treatments, diet, exercise and even guardian angels and past lives than the parts of you that have been damaged by other people or have even been the root of self-inflicted damage themselves. However, the 'serious student' knows that sooner or later the reptiles won't be defeated by anything other than an eye-to-eye confrontation.

The other thing to bear in mind when you go in search of those implicit languages or 'reptiles' is that *they are not representative of the real you*. They are just deeply embedded learned responses that you developed to keep you safe, and as with all fears the longer you avoid facing them the worse they get and the more they control your life. Yes, there really is no doubt that to live the life you long to live, these dark, shadowy feelings that are embedded in your subconscious must be released, because they are like poison in your system and will do you great harm in the end.

> *'One does not become enlightened by imagining figures of light, but by making the darkness conscious.'* – Carl Jung

Why Hasn't this Been Explained to Me Before?

Apart from the depth of honesty and humility required, another reason why implicit languages are so hard to get your head around is because they are so ambiguous. Feelings are so open to interpretation or misinterpretation. They can't be pigeon-holed or labelled because they are so unique to each individual. You can't test them scientifically in a laboratory because you will never get the same result twice. So no one can give you a formula for understanding your own feelings, because the stimulus that you have been exposed to and the way you respond to it, from the moment you were conceived to now, is entirely unique to you and you alone.

> *People are so intimidated and frightened by the uncertainty of feelings.*

We are also living at a time when our feelings are becoming harder and harder to connect with. We are surrounded by weapons of mass *distraction* that over-stimulate our minds and bodies so when it comes to identifying the subtlety of how we feel, it is practically impossible. We are constantly looking for fulfilment externally through material possessions, exciting relationships, jobs and careers, fast-paced films or music, etc., so that when we don't get the same instant and obvious gratification by looking internally we feel deeply isolated and unfulfilled.

However, the irony is that being able to connect congruently with our feelings (our implicit languages) is actually the fulfilment that every human being on the planet is looking for. This is because connecting congruently with our feelings (our implicit languages) allows us to be understood, and when we are understood by ourselves and others, we feel safe.

Chapter 3
I Am the Traumatic Memories I Release

'Inside of a ring or out, ain't nothing wrong with going down. It's staying down that's wrong.' – Muhammad Ali

I believe that the information you are about to read in this chapter (when combined with the other insights I share in this book) contains some of the most valuable information you will ever read in your life. It will explain, in the most simple and straightforward ways possible, some of the reasons why you may feel stuck and unable to make changes. This groundbreaking knowledge has come to me through my own understanding of how the subconscious works and through the study of experts like Dr Peter Levine and Dr Robert Scaer in the fields of trauma-release.

So get ready for some major light-bulb moments, as you find out why healing your life is near impossible if you have stored trauma in your mind and body.

What Is Trauma?

So, first of all, what do I mean by trauma? This term needs clarification because it does have the potential to be overused in our modern world. Perhaps you have even heard people say statements like, 'I have had such a traumatic day with the kids today,' when really these people are experiencing stress rather than trauma.

> *It is important to recognise that, while every traumatic event is stressful, not every stressful event is traumatic.* – Dr Peter Levine

That said, I define trauma as a deeply disturbing experience where the individual perceives that their life is at threat or the situation they are in is inescapable. It is crucial to recognise that we don't have to experience a near-fatal accident to become traumatised; trauma occurs through our *perception* of events (either, objectively, minor or monumental). The key to remember when you are considering if an experience you have had was traumatic is: Did you feel the situation you were in was inescapable to the degree that you feared the next moment?

For example, it is not unusual for people to be traumatised in childhood by a teacher or a parent chastising them inappropriately. As always in life, the specifics of what happens to us are not as important as how we respond.

> *If the individual feels that their life is at threat or they cannot escape, the potential for trauma is present.*

It's also important to recognise that experiencing trauma is a natural part of life, and unless we are wrapped in cotton wool from birth to death it is highly likely that we will all encounter it in one way or another. In fact, when the process of experiencing trauma – and, crucially, releasing it – has been fully experienced and completed, it actually has the potential to make you stronger and more resilient. However, it is my experience that more and more people are experiencing trauma and storing it, and when we don't release trauma from our minds and bodies, this has a negative impact on our whole lives.

Releasing trauma from our minds and our bodies actually has the potential to make us more resilient. Resilience relates to our ability to recover, and in some cases come back stronger than before.

The Freeze Response and Trauma

It is well known that when our lives are in danger we go into the fight-or-flight response, where massive biochemical changes happen in the body/mind to help us either run away or confront danger. However, now we are beginning to understand what happens to the body/mind when danger is still present and one or both of those responses has been suppressed and/or ineffectively utilised: the body/mind goes into the freeze response. As the name suggests, when this happens the body/mind is frozen in time.

The 'freeze response' is Nature's final protection mechanism.
It switches off pain and suffering from the body/mind.

A good example of this in the natural world is a rabbit caught in headlights. Fight or flight has been ineffective, so the only option left is to freeze. If the wheels of the car miss the animal and it survives, it would then complete the freeze response process by finding a safe place to 'shake it out'.

> *The shaking aspect is so important because it simulates the act of escape and erases the procedural memory of not being able to escape.*

In an ideal world, humans would allow the same process to take place: after the danger has passed and the realisation of survival has returned, the individual would go through a significant shaking process to release the freeze response naturally. However, this process can be easily interrupted in today's modern and overly sympathetic world (often by the individual's conscious desire to override it, or even by well-meaning people who try to stop the shaking prematurely, sometimes with drugs). If this happens the trauma can become frozen in the individual's system.

How Trauma Is Stored: A Summary
1. *The fight-or-flight response has been suppressed or utilised ineffectively.*
2. *The freeze response has been triggered because the individual feels that their life is in danger and/or they can't escape.*
3. *The freeze response process has not been completed (that is, little or no shaking has*

occurred after the event, either because it has been interrupted in some way or the individual has overridden the desire to do so).

My Story – A Trauma from My Childhood

To give you an example of how I was able to build resilience through trauma, I want to share the story of how I almost lost one of my eyes. I was about 12 years old and one sunny weekend myself and two of my friends had either been allowed out to play or had escaped from the orphanage – I can't remember which scenario was true, but either way we were enjoying some much-needed freedom from the strict rule of the nuns. So, as rather naïve and foolish boys do, we headed off to explore the nearby railway line. Thankfully my accident didn't involve any of the obvious dangers, or I might not be here now to tell the tale, but it did involve another older boy who had the reputation of being a bully. This boy didn't like the idea of me and my two friends on his 'turf', so decided to chase us away. As we ran off into the distance he decided to throw quite a sizeable lump of rock in my direction, just as I looked round to see how far away we were from him. The pain and fear I felt instantly as the rock made contact with my eye was indescribable, and was probably made worse because I had no reference point of having a parent nearby to make me feel safe. For reasons I will explain later in this chapter, my memory of the next few hours is incoherent, but I do remember being rushed to hospital and being examined by very anxious doctors who were extremely worried that they might have to completely remove my eye. It was a terrifying time and I was without

continued

doubt in the freeze response, as both my fight and flight responses had been triggered ineffectively and now I was in a situation that was inescapable. However, looking back now at such a traumatic experience with the knowledge I am sharing with you in this book, I can't help but wonder if the gods were watching over me that day, because for some unknown reason the wise, clever doctors in the hospital decided not to operate or administer any strong drugs. They said they wouldn't do anything for 24 hours, as they wanted to give my body the opportunity to heal. So what did my body do? Yes, that's right, it shook. I can still remember lying in the hospital bed on a warm day covered in blankets while I trembled and shivered with complete and utter shock. I now understand that this was my mind and body simulating the escape I had been trying make so that the memory of the trauma did not become stored in my mind and body. Miraculously, my eye did heal and I know that I became a stronger and more resilient person because of the ordeal I completed. Although they never found the bully who threw the rock, from that day on I never ran away from bullies again and I became someone who learned how to deal with that particular archetype appropriately. Although I do still wear glasses today as a result of the 'traumatic cataract' I was left with, I firmly believe that the age-old saying is true: 'What doesn't kill you makes you stronger.'

Please note that I am sharing this story as an example of how the freeze response process was allowed to complete naturally and helped me build resilience. I am not suggesting that every individual should be treated in the same way, as every case of trauma is completely unique.

How Can You Tell If Trauma Is Stored in the Body/Mind?

There are many signs that trauma has been stored in the body/mind, and this list is certainly not exhaustive, but the key factor that all of these signs have in common is that they help the individual to avoid re-experiencing the perceived horror of their inescapable trauma again.

However, the irony of this protection mechanism is that what we are fearing we are actually creating, what we are resisting is actually persisting. When we avoid, fear or resist anything in life, we are actually just prolonging the agony. To release trauma we must gently and intelligently enter into it, fully and completely.

Here are some of the signs that trauma may be stored in the body/mind ... but before you study them, please bear in mind that this list is not exhaustive and there are other conditions/illnesses/diseases that some of these symptoms can relate to as well. These signs are not exclusive to people who have experienced trauma, but hopefully the list that follows can help to guide your own trauma-identification process in an empowering way.

- Cognitive processes are inhibited when trauma is stored in the body/mind, so you may find it difficult to think deeply/clearly or take on new information.

- You may feel tired all the time, have trouble sleeping or experience insomnia.

- You may experience anxiety and/or panic attacks.

- You may experience involuntary body movements (minor shakes, tics) that may or may not be noticeable to you.

- You may display signs of exaggerated eye movements that are noticeable to others.

- Your senses (including tolerances to certain foods) may become over- or under-sensitive.

- You may become either overly controlling or overly passive.

- You may overreact to life events/situations.

- You may misinterpret information/misread situations, which can create conflict in your life.

- You may have pains in your body that can't be accounted for.

- You may experience mild or even severe states of disassociation. Disassociation is where you detach from your physical and/or emotional reality.

- People who have stored trauma in their body/mind may also find it very difficult to keep their body/mind still because the procedural memory of not being able to escape is still active.

> *Procedural memory is a type of long-term memory that resides below conscious awareness. You are using procedural memory to understand the meaning of the words you are reading now. When trauma is stored in the body/mind, your procedural memory of trying to escape is still active. So it doesn't matter if you experienced trauma ten days ago, ten months ago or even ten or more years ago; if you haven't released it from your body/mind, the subconscious memory of the trauma is still having an impact on you today.*

Numbing the Pain

You'll notice that, with the possible exception of disassociation, most of the signs of 'stored trauma' that I have listed involve elements of body and/or mind arousal. The body/mind is in motion, in pain, busy, overactive, and this can be explained in more detail, because these reactions aren't just related to the active procedural memory which I have already explained.

Another reason why we don't stop or relax when we have stored trauma is because when we are active we produce endorphins. Most of us know this to be the case because this information is used by health professionals to encourage us to take moderate exercise.

However, when trauma is stored in the body/mind, the individual very often becomes *over*active. This can take the form of excessive exercising, a constantly busy work/family schedule or other activities that keep the body/mind frantically distracted. There is a biological reason for this, because, as mentioned, overactivity produces endorphins. These are similar in effect to the drug morphine. So the individual who is always on the go is actually programming their body/mind to keep producing a morphine-like substance to numb the emotional and/or physical pain of the embedded trauma.

So although the individual isn't consciously injecting themselves with strong painkillers, their overly active behaviour is subconsciously triggering the body's natural pharmacy into action and, as with synthetic drugs, there are side-effects as a result of this behaviour. The main side-effect of producing morphine-like endorphins through prolonged overactivity is the impairment of cognitive ability. Very often the individual is unable to think deeply or clearly when they create this internal response, much as would happen if they had they injected themselves with a pharmaceutical painkiller.

The other side-effect is that the body/mind is always out of balance, because humans were never designed to respond to trauma in this way over such an extended period of time.

It is also worth noting that the behaviour of the overly-active individual is also very disruptive for other people to be around. Although they can't see it themselves, their constant state of overactivity has an impact on partners, children, friends and work colleagues. If the people around the individual are not strong, or are in their developmental stages, they are likely to develop health conditions and/or behavioural problems themselves, meaning that the effects of even one person's trauma can be widespread.

How We Remember Trauma

What happens if we can't remember the details of the trauma we have experienced? Perhaps we disassociated before or during the event? Maybe we were traumatised in childhood before we learned to speak? It might even be that we have since blocked these hugely influential memories out of our minds. Again, let me be very clear about this: even if you can't consciously remember a trauma you've experienced, it will still be having an impact on your subconscious.

It may also be interesting for you to learn that it is perfectly normal for you not to have a sequential memory of traumatic events. As I explained in the story about my eye, my recollection of that experience is very incoherent. When I remember it, I don't see it as a complete motion picture or film in my mind's eye. I see it more as snapshots or stills. Some of the frames are clearer than others. Some are black and white. Some are colour. Some have associated sounds, smells, tastes. Others don't. I believe the reason for this is, again, Nature's wonderful protection mechanism. To me it makes total sense that our memories are 'censored' through disassociation so that we are never given more than we can handle.

However, what if you can't remember a thing yet you intuitively know that you have been traumatised? Well, there are still ways of working to rebalance your body/mind without having to revisit your experiences. It is important to stress, though, that releasing specific traumas is a specialised area and should not be undertaken without the guidance of a professional in this field.

The Compulsion to Re-experience Trauma

Another fascinating element of trauma is that, if we have not released it from our body/mind, we can be compelled to keep re-experiencing the effects of it.

The commonsense answer for why we do this is that when trauma becomes stored, as we now know we go into the freeze response, so our *behaviour* can also become frozen in time along with our body/mind. So we keep responding in the same way, feeling the same way, acting the same way, as we did just before, during or after the trauma because we haven't completed the process at a subconscious level. As a result we are drawn into situations that keep repeating the effects of the original trauma in a subconscious attempt finally to complete the entire process so it can be released.

This can be a very difficult concept for people to understand, but I must stress again that this happening at a level below conscious awareness. The good news is that becoming aware of patterns in your life that involve events, accidents, even people and relationships, can help you become aware of any unresolved trauma that you may have.

> *When you release trauma, your behaviour changes.*
> *Changes in behaviour bring changes in your life.*

The Cultural Cage

Understanding that we feel trapped in what can only be described as a cage may also help you become aware of unresolved trauma at a deeper level.

Before I explain further, you may be having trouble imagining a human being inside a cage. Well, that may be because you are thinking too literally. We may not be surrounded by metal bars with locks on but, like it or not, most of humanity (yes, including people who aren't even in jail) are existing within the parameters of a 'cultural cage'.

Our cultural cage, as I touched on at the beginning of this book, has been set up to adhere to the constructs of the ego. To briefly recap, the ego has four main beliefs which are all centred around the idea of GETTING. More things. More status. More respect. More, more, more. These beliefs are:

1. I am what I have.

2. I am what I do.

3. I am what other people think of me.

4. I am separate from everyone else.

Now, when we live in ego-consciousness, life is all about competition and not cooperation, so after a certain amount of time there comes a point when this is no longer sustainable. This is the reality we face in our 'cultural cage': too many people feel trapped by the beliefs of the ego and, as a result, are looking for ways to become free again.

This is especially relevant to trauma because (unlike animals living in the wild) domesticated animals, animals kept in zoos, and indeed human beings are more likely to store trauma because they are kept in cages. It stands to reason that if a living creature feels trapped, it stores any feelings that it is unable to express freely.

How to Release Trauma

First, as this area of work is relatively new and utterly unique in each case, I am unable to explain many of the complex processes that I am aware of to guide someone through trauma-release; however, I will be detailing some ideas later in this book that everyone can follow to develop their healing potential in general.

Having said that, I would also like to make it clear again that the power of simply acknowledging this information at a very deep level should never, ever, ever be underestimated. All too often I meet people who just want the answers without doing any of the research. I have been in situations where I have explained this knowledge to people, only for them to say 'OK, so now what do I do about it?' without even giving themselves time to blink their eyes. This 'I want my life fixed in a second' approach is a consequence of our modern world where we can have what we want when we want – but when it comes to healing our minds, bodies and spirits, it is a very foolish position to take. When we just want to get to the answers, we miss out on the experience of learning, and gaining wisdom is a fundamental part of being human.

The information in this chapter took me decades to acquire to the level that I understand and apply it today, and I would suggest that if you are serious about your healing journey you will have to become someone who researches your own life with a fine-tooth comb in the same way that I did. The clear and concise information that you have just read is not intended to give you all the answers to solving your life, but it will give you a head start. So the first step is to *acknowledge* this information, sit with it, contemplate it, study it, observe it, learn from it.

> 'We can't change what we don't acknowledge.' –
> Dr Phil McGraw

I have thought about, reflected on, read and re-read this chapter from many different perspectives and I believe that whether you have experienced trauma from physical, emotional or sexual abuse, from surgery, from an accident, from the birthing process, from watching someone you love die, from the horrors of war, from being abandoned, betrayed or humiliated, the universal information in this chapter can really begin to help you move forward ... and the first step to doing that is to absorb all of the new realisations you have just been given at a very deep level.

I will add, finally, that it is crucial that you feel safe and secure with these new thoughts, so be kind to yourself in this process of understanding and constantly affirm to your body/mind that your natural state is health. Always remember that the more you enter into your emotions with honesty and integrity, the more you emerge with strength, resilience and that all-important feeling of inner safety.

Chapter 4

How to Move Forward: Five 'I Am Healing' Behaviours

'Teachers open the door. You enter by yourself.'
– Chinese proverb

It is my belief that the information I have shared with you in this book has the potential to connect you with your subconscious programming like never before.

This connection is so important, because healing is not a conscious process. Think about the cut on your finger that heals with no conscious intervention from you. Healing is a *subconscious* process and is brought about by a much greater force than our conscious minds. However, when we remove our subconscious barriers, by consciously understanding who we are and why we do what we do, we become more receptive and open to healing.

It goes without saying, though, that understanding ourselves is only part of the story, because we must also work tirelessly to let go of the subconscious programmes that are no longer working for us. With this in mind I have compiled five 'I Am Healing' behaviours for you to adopt. These behaviours, when activated, will assist you in allowing your subconscious barriers to be released.

You may be someone who thinks that these behaviours should include daily rituals of drinking a certain amount of water, eating the right quota of fruit and vegetables and making sure you exercise. While all of these behaviours are important, I want to offer you some new ideas that work alongside commonsense thinking but stretch your mind, body and spirit at the same time. It also goes without saying that the behaviours I have compiled are certainly not the definitive list, but they are excellent starting points.

So I believe these five healing behaviours have the potential to begin to transform your mind, body and spirit to a state of harmony and balance, and allow you to become much more receptive and open to healing. However, I have not gone into great detail about *how* you activate each of these behaviours, because it is my experience that setting out strict structures or rigid disciplines very rarely works long term. My approach is always to empower people with knowledge of *what* needs to be done and the specifics of *how* you do it; from there it is up to you. It is your life path and you must always ask for guidance from people you trust if and when you need it.

Having said that, I have listed 'Questions for Reflection' after each of the healing behaviours, which I hope will help you to consolidate the learning and think deeply about each one. These are questions that require a lot of time, energy and thought to answer honestly. There are no right or wrong answers to these questions and they can be returned to regularly as your experiences change, but it is important to pay very close attention to them because they have the power to create new thoughts and feelings for you at a very deep level.

Words Don't Teach – Experience Does

It is also important to point out that, as you read through these behaviours, it is highly likely that you will feel like a lot of information is missing. There is every chance that the voice inside your head will keep saying, 'Yes, I understand, but how do I bring this behaviour to life?' That is exactly the experience I want you to have, because if I gave you all the solutions without you having to make any effort, you wouldn't value them. This is because words don't teach; experience teaches. The purpose of this information is to make you more efficient, so that you are aware of the destinations for healing. How you get to each destination, the journeys, if you like, are yours.

A good analogy might be to think of a mathematical equation. I am offering you the idea that '4' is one of the answers you could look for, but how you get to '4' is down to you. You might decide that 2+2 is the best way, or 1+3 or even 0+4. There may even be a few times when you feel that you have got the numbers all wrong, but the act of doing the sums and metaphorically scratching your head will teach you far more than blindly reading any amount of formulae I could cram into this book. The exciting thing is you now don't have any excuses not to start 'working it out' ... especially when your healing depends on it.

You'll notice that I have formulated these behaviours around 'I Am' constructions, because, as you will discover in the final chapter, when you use the words 'I Am' you set in motion an inherent power within yourself. The words 'I Am' leave no room for hesitancy or doubt. These behaviours are not passive affirmations for you to say mindlessly in front of a mirror three times every day; these behaviours are just that, *behaviours*, which means they require action. So you don't just read them, you say them, you feel them, you do them, and ultimately you become them consciously and subconsciously.

Healing Behaviour #1
I Am Expanding
My Awareness

*'And those who were seen dancing were thought insane
by those who could not hear the music.'*
– Friedrich Nietzsche

What does it mean to expand your awareness? Expanding your awareness means to become more aware of who you are and the world around you – and just when you think you've become more aware, you become more aware again, and so on and so on.

A good analogy is to think of looking at a tree. From a distance, you can make out the shape of the trunk and the green foliage, but that's about it. As you walk closer you become more aware of the branches, and you might even see a few birds flying in and out of their nests. Closer still and you can touch the grooves of the dark brown bark and walk on the thick chunky roots which are pushing up through the ground. You might even, as you stand underneath the canopy, look at the tiny, almost transparent veins on a leaf and wonder how they help to nourish the tree with rainwater. At first glance the tree was just a tree, but by the time you have finished experiencing it, you are far more connected, far more informed, far more aware – not just about the tree but about yourself.

The quote that opens this section could also be thought of in the same way. Imagine looking at a group of people from a distance and seeing them jumping about, waving their arms and shaking their heads. You might think, as you look on in silence, that these people have totally lost their minds, but as you walk closer you hear the music and you begin to experience the truth. Again you feel more connected, more informed, more aware of other people and yourself.

Expanding my own awareness was a behaviour that came very naturally to me, though I don't really understand why. As a young boy in Ireland I was curious about everyone I met, right down to the way they smiled. As an engineer I had to understand hugely complicated circuits, right down to the tiniest components. As an author of self-development books I have to make sense of the complexities of human behaviour, right down to subtleties of the languages we speak. I have done all of these things by looking at the bigger picture first (as with the tree analogy) and then becoming more and more aware of and experiencing the finer detail.

Incredibly, when you do this you start to notice universal patterns, principles, symbols and themes. You start to become aware that true knowledge isn't conceptual, intellectual, theory or belief-based. You start to understand that there is in fact one ubiquitous source of all knowledge, and all you have to do to tap into it is become aware, acutely aware, of your own experiences.

> *There is a root from which all knowledge has emerged, and humanity has many names for it. In Greek it is called* gnosis. *The higher meaning of gnosis is 'knowledge from experience'. In Tibet it is called* rigpa *(knowing), and the Sanskrit term is* Jna *(knowledge).*

You may be thinking, this is all very well and good, but how will expanding my awareness help me heal? The answer is very simple: when you expand your awareness, you start to uncover *gnosis*, which ultimately leads you to the truth – and as the saying goes, the truth will set you free.

Having said that, the process of expanding your awareness is not an easy thing to do, and is not a task that should be entered into lightly. The truth *will* set you free but, trust me, not everyone wants to hear it – and that could even include you. There will be times when you will feel misunderstood, alone and confused, but remember that everything that you are experiencing which brings out a reaction in you is simply a reflection of a part of yourself.

> *'There is no coming to consciousness without pain.'*
> – Carl Jung

So if you are serious about healing, put all your beliefs to one side, along with everything you have intellectually learned, and expand your awareness about you and the world around you. Look at the big picture, focus on the finer detail, discover knowledge through experience and be the one who dances to the music that no one else can hear.

Questions for Reflection

- What beliefs do I have that are not based on my experiences? How much more aware would I become of the truth if I began to release the beliefs that I haven't experienced?

- To what extent do I observe my own behaviour? How much more aware would I become if I were able to observe my behaviour at a deeper level?

- How deeply do I look for patterns, principles, symbols and themes in my life? How much more aware would I become if I started to look for these truths in my life?

- How dedicated am I to searching for the truth? How much more aware would I become if I were always in search of truth?

- What part of my life would begin to heal if I focused on gaining knowledge through experience? How much more aware would I be about healing myself and others if I had experienced it myself?

An Exercise to Try

A wonderful exercise to help you begin to expand your awareness is prefrontal cortex tapping. This is a technique I have been developing and using for several years. The prefrontal cortex, as you have already found out earlier in this book, is a region of the brain that deals with reason and logic, or what is sometimes referred to in psychology as 'executive function'. Interestingly, modern research is now discovering that people who were brought up in environments where they didn't feel emotionally or physically safe have prefrontal cortexes that are underdeveloped. As mentioned earlier, in the case of the prefrontal cortex the term 'underdeveloped' doesn't mean big or small. It relates to the density of that region of the brain.

With all of this in mind, it is my experience that gently tapping all over the forehead where the prefrontal cortex is located is an incredibly beneficial thing to do. I believe that it helps to expand awareness because it induces a state of calm. This is important because when we are calm we are able to absorb new information much more efficiently. We are also experiencing touch when we do any type of tapping, which stimulates the healing systems in our body/mind. Tapping also creates tiny electrical impulses which allow energetic blockages to be released from the body/mind. Can you imagine how much more receptive you would be to *gnosis* if you were to make prefrontal cortex tapping part of your daily routine?

It can be done with two or more fingers over a five-minute period once or twice a day while saying the following statement: *Even though my prefrontal cortex hasn't developed because I have been living in fear, I now choose to allow my prefrontal cortex to develop.*

You don't have to use these exact words, but it is important that any statement that you do use has the three elements of *acknowledging* that your prefrontal cortex hasn't developed in density, *explaining* why your prefrontal cortex hasn't developed in density, and *affirming* what you now want to do about it.

I also find it very beneficial to take a few deep breaths after each round of tapping, making sure that I exhale very slowly and consciously. It really is a wonderful new-thinking relaxation aid that has helped me to expand my awareness in so many ways. I hope you will find it as valuable as I have.

Healing Behaviour #2
I Am Connected to My Physical Body

'If anything is sacred, the human body is sacred.'
– Walt Whitman

The more I learn about human behaviour in the modern Western world, the more I am coming to realise how disconnected we have become from our physical presence. It astounds me when I ask people to tell me how they feel, or ask them where in their body they can experience a certain thought, and they stare blankly back at me and say 'I don't know.'

There are various reasons why people disconnect from their physical body, and many of those reasons usually come under the umbrella of trauma. This is because when we experience trauma we disassociate, believing subconsciously that this will protect us from reliving the horror of such an event again. Of course this safety mechanism is hopelessly flawed as a long-term solution, because when we disconnect from our bodies we are ignoring our internal guidance systems, which actually help to keep us safe in the first place.

Becoming reacquainted with your physical body can be a slow and sometimes frightening process for some people, especially if they have been physically or sexually abused, but this healing behaviour can be animated in your own time and in your own way. There is no rush, there are also no right or wrong answers, and there is no ultimate goal to achieve.

On the other hand, you may be someone reading this now who thinks you are already perfectly connected with your body. As always, I'd like you to go deeper and remember that there is always more to discover, more to learn. I'd like you to consider that learning the language of the body is much like learning a foreign language, so even if you know the basics, you could always become aware of the more advanced grammar, the syntax and the idioms.

When you are connected with your body you have a strong sense of your personal power, so you don't have irrational fears about your physical or material survival. You know what you need to do to make a living, you know discernment when it comes to the foods you eat and the fluids you drink, you know whom to build relationships with, you feel confident about restoring your own health and wellbeing without the need of unnecessary medications or surgeries, and you know all of these things (and more) because your thoughts are in tune with your feelings. You are responding to how your body feels at a deep level rather than having knee-jerk reactions to the first seductive thought that flashes into your mind.

There is no strict formula to reconnecting with the feelings in your body. The process is utterly unique to each individual. For example, the martial art of Aikido taught me lots of techniques to enhance my bodily feelings, but I also learned how to do this just by becoming aware of how important feelings are. I truly believe that once you become open to something, the solutions will materialise. Once you ask the questions, the answers do come. When the student is ready, the teacher appears.

With all this in mind, you may be interested to know that I have compiled various relaxation and meditation audios, some of which focus on reconnecting you with your feelings in your body. These are available on my website www.thewysecentre.co.uk. Again, I hope you will find the tools that I am providing useful, because I cannot stress strongly enough that the happiest, healthiest and probably most fulfilled people I have met in my life have all been people who were connected with the feelings they experience in their physical body.

Questions for Reflection

- To what extent do I listen and respond to the feelings I get in my body? How could I get better at listening and responding to my feelings?

- How safe do I feel in my physical body? How could I make myself feel safer in my physical body?

- To what extent do I consult the physical sensations in my body when I am making choices? How could I get better at consulting the physical sensations in my body when I am making choices?

- How connected am I to the physical sensations that other people might have in their bodies when they are around me? What benefits would there be for me if I could tune in to the physical sensations that other people are having in my presence?

- How would my healing progress if I felt safe with my feelings and had a healthy understanding of my personal power? How can I continue to use my feelings to understand my personal power?

Healing Behaviour #3
I Am Getting to Know My Subconscious

'Until you make the unconscious conscious, it will direct your life and you will call it fate.' – Carl Jung

'Know thyself' is a sacred command, and is probably one of the most difficult tasks any person could undertake. This is because you think that you know yourself already: you know your name, your know your shoe size, you know your address, what else is there to know? Well, when it comes to healing, there is a hell of a lot more.

You see, most people know consciously how they operate, and although the conscious mind has many uses, it is very limited when it comes to knowing yourself. The conscious mind is where you reason, logic and plan. The conscious mind is where you tell yourself stories about who you are, and as a result the conscious mind is the biggest hurdle you will have to overcome when it comes to getting to know yourself at a deep and meaningful level.

A good metaphor would be to think of a bowl, covered with a lid on a table in a restaurant. None of the diners really knows what is in that bowl, and everyone wonders about the contents within. Even the bowl can't explain what's inside, because bowls can't speak, of course. As the night goes on, the restaurant gets busier and busier, and inevitably someone jostles the bowl and the contents spill out everywhere. Now everyone knows what was inside the bowl. Human beings have the ability to be like the bowl with the unknown contents, and when they are jostled they show what they have inside. They show the contents and character that were once invisible.

This is because when an event takes us by surprise or puts us under pressure, our conscious mind is unable to supply us with a quick enough response. Our conscious mind wants to make sense of everything, which is a slow, methodical process, so when we are caught off-guard the immediate reactions – which we learned during our formative years – surface from our subconscious. If we are serious about getting to know ourselves, it is these reactions that will give us the answers we so desperately need.

OK, you might be thinking, that's easy to address. I will just become more aware of my reactions when I'm taken by surprise or put under pressure. That *will* help, but only up to point, because again you will be relying too much on the conscious mind to solve problems that are beyond its capacity. Some of the events that 'jostle' you in your life aren't even obvious to your conscious mind. Sometimes you don't even know when you've been 'jostled', but your subconscious knows everything and will create solutions based on how it has been programmed.

Now, don't misunderstand me. I have met and worked with people who have displayed the most wonderful subconscious reactions when they have been caught off-guard. I have seen characteristics such as loyalty, kindness, compassion and generosity come to the surface in individuals during some of the most difficult circumstances, so I am not saying that everyone's subconscious programming is corrupt; far from it. I am just suggesting that if you are serious about healing, you need to make sure that you are doing everything you possibly can to respond with healthy characteristics in every and all situations.

As I explained at the beginning of this chapter, this is probably one of the most arduous journeys that any human being embarks on, because so often you have to shine a light on the darkness and search out something that is, in effect, completely invisible to you. You have to break the cycle of denial that you have lived in for so many years and you have to get really honest with yourself, at a subconscious level, about what you need to change to make your life and other people's lives better.

I must stress, though, that you don't have to 'beat yourself up' or 'torture' yourself in order to know yourself at a deeper level. You do, however, have to learn a quality that is seen as a virtue in all spiritual traditions. That quality is humility. Again, 'easy', you might think, 'I can be humble,' but it is my experience that for so many people the process of life subconsciously teaches them that humility leads to humiliation and, trust me, most human beings will do whatever it takes to avoid the feeling of humiliation.

So with that in mind, let me explain the difference between the two feelings. This I hope will be beneficial for you to keep in mind on your journey of self-discovery, because if you are consciously aware of the confusion that most people feel about these two feelings, you can learn and grow.

Humiliation makes you feel as if your rank, prestige or self-esteem has been lowered, and it relates to the ego. Humility makes you feel modest, respectful and grateful, and relates to the soul. When you are reflecting on a situation where you subconsciously responded in an unhealthy way, I would urge you to ask yourself if you are feeling humiliated by the situation which has now stopped you in your tracks, or if you feel humility for a situation which could allow you to grow.

How do you know if your subconscious has responded in an unhealthy way? Look at the state of your relationships, your finances and your health. There are clues everywhere.

Questions for Reflection

- To what extent am I aware of the unhealthy subconscious characteristics that surface in me when I am caught off-guard or put under pressure?

- What subconscious characteristics am I proud of? Can I remember occasions when I was put under pressure and caught off-guard and responded healthily with a deeply embedded behaviour? How can those healthy characteristics help me address the unhealthy ones?

- How honest am I about areas in my life where I don't feel fulfilled, and what impact is my deeply embedded and subconscious denial having on my circumstances?

- To what extent do I understand the difference between the feelings of humility and the feelings of humiliation? What experiences can I remember where I confused the two feelings?

- How much more deeply could I begin to know myself?

Healing Behaviour #4
I Am Silent

'All man's miseries derive from not being able to sit quietly in a room alone.' – Blaise Pascal

As you read the words on this page you'll notice the spaces between them. If you look even closer you will notice the even smaller spaces between the letters; closer still and you'll notice the spaces that help to make the shape of each of the letters as well. It is these spaces that help everything to make sense. The same can be said of music: it is the spaces between the musical notes that actually create the song. Without the spaces, all you would hear is one long continuous note.

I'm sharing this with you because human beings also need space to allow us to make sense of our lives, and this space comes in the form of silence at both an external and internal level.

Let me explain. First we are able to experience external silence when we disconnect from the noisy world around us. We are able to sit in a quiet place and contemplate our thoughts without the distraction of other sounds, such as moving traffic, barking dogs, ringing phones, chattering people, loud televisions, blaring radios and so on. This level of silence is a fundamental need of the human condition, and even if we are foolish enough not to make an effort to connect with it during our hours of consciousness, we certainly connect with it effortlessly when we sleep. Sleep allows us to enter deep states of external silence, and you won't find a doctor or a scientist on the planet who would deny the enormous health benefits that it brings.

External silence allows us to release stress and anxiety, and when we release stress and anxiety we are more receptive to learning, growing and finding answers. And when we learn, grow and find answers, we begin to heal.

The problem we face in today's Western world is that external noise is the norm, and for some people external silence can even be terrifying. So many of us now belong to a culture that has become subconsciously addicted to distractions, so actually hearing or listening to nothing can be emotionally painful. This is because it when it is quiet on the outside, you are able to hear the thoughts within ... which leads me on to internal silence.

Internal silence is when we are able to find the space between our thoughts, and it takes a lot of time, patience and practice to master. This is because sometimes our thoughts can be as loud and as busy as the noises we hear externally, like the phones ringing or the radio blaring. As a result it can be much easier to ignore our thoughts rather than stop, observe them, reflect on them and contemplate them, let alone go on to release them and find the space between them!

Some people call the art of mastering internal silence 'meditation', and for those who have experienced it, it can be profoundly life-changing. Being able to disconnect from external noise is one thing, and it is very beneficial, but being able to disconnect from internal noise and experience silence within is simply serene. If you have ever seen someone meditate you will be aware that they don't fall asleep; they are fully conscious inside but they seem to almost energetically leave their bodies, and when they 'return' they are fully refreshed and invigorated. Often in their silent space they have found answers to problems they needed, healed an ache or a pain, or simply felt the joy of being fully present. People who meditate regularly find it much easier to connect with themselves, with other people and with the process of life. For these reasons and many, many others, I firmly believe it is an essential life skill that must be formally introduced into our education system so that it becomes the new norm for generations to come. In the meantime each of us can make a conscious effort to be that change we want to see in the world and do it for ourselves.

There have been countless books written about meditation and the benefits it brings, so I won't go into too much detail, as this is your silent journey to explore. I just wanted to encourage you to start to think generally about silence at an external and internal level so that you can begin to do whatever it takes to introduce it into your life.

The most important thing to remember is that it does take practice and it isn't something you can master overnight. For that reason I have created a variety of relaxation and meditation audios to help you attune your body/mind to the frequency of silence (see my website www.thewysecentre.co.uk). Many of these recordings contain positive subliminal messages and unique language patterns and communication structures so that you can begin to access silence subconsciously as well as consciously.

So, in closing, if you are able to work continually at animating this healing behaviour in a way that feels right for you, there is no doubt in my mind that you will reap wonderful rewards (although, crucially, you mustn't make that a goal; the rewards are simply a by-product). I know this to be true because every experience that I have had in my life has become richer from connecting with silence, and everything that has ever been created in your life and the world around us has been created from silence ... this last fact alone is surely enough to move anyone to silence?

Questions for Reflection

- To what extent do I make a conscious effort to connect with external silence every day? How can I make more of an effort so that external silence eventually comes naturally to me?

- What feelings go through my body/mind when I experience external silence?

- If my thoughts were external noises, how loud or quiet would they be? How mindful am I of how noisy or quiet my thoughts are?

- How often do I talk about my problems with others rather than enter into silence by myself for answers?

- What amazing things have I created in my life from silence? What else could I create if I were able to utilise the power of external and internal silence?

Healing Behaviour #5
I Am Devoted to Seeking Truth

'Rather than love, than money, than fame, give me truth.' – Henry David Thoreau

When was the last time you used or even heard the word 'devoted'? When was the last time you felt devotion? Devotion is about having an eternal, selfless affection for something or someone, and it is a feeling that perhaps we have lost sight of in our world of quick-fixes and disposability.

You see, devotion isn't something you can pick up and put down when it suits you. It isn't something that comes and goes. It isn't something that you enter into with any thought about your own personal gain. It isn't something that has rules attached. It isn't about achieving a goal. It isn't something you even consciously choose. You are either devoted or you aren't. There is no in-between.

Why are you devoted? You just are. That's it. Full stop.

So, with all that in mind, can you imagine now how it might feel to become someone who is devoted to seeking truth in any and all situations? Now, I understand the gravity of the concept I am suggesting, because truth is also a feeling like no other and perhaps one that we have also lost sight of in our world of entitlements and judgements. In fact, when you think about it, truth is very similar to devotion in lots of ways.

You can't pick it up and put it down when it suits you. Truth isn't something that comes and goes. It isn't something that you enter into with any thought about your own personal gain. It isn't something that has rules attached. It isn't about achieving a goal. It isn't something you even consciously choose. It is either truth or it isn't. There is no in-between. Sound familiar?

So you can see why becoming someone who is devoted to seeking truth is a massive undertaking. To be someone who is devoted to seeking out truth about their life and life in general is, without doubt, a gargantuan task – but as the Chinese philosopher Lao Tzu said, the journey of a thousand miles begins with a single step. Just bear in mind, though, as you take the first few steps, that in the beginning the answers you find may make you more confused – but ultimately your devotion will reveal truth in everything, everywhere.

How will you know when you find truth? The answer to that is very simple: you will know when you find truth because it silences you. People who know truth can't speak about it, they can't chatter it away, they can't manipulate it. People who know truth can only observe and experience it, because if they try to explain it or justify it to others who have no point of reference for it, it becomes too complex. Truth is always revealed to you in a way that stops you in your tracks. So if you were to try and give it away, you would create an even bigger problem either for yourself or somebody you love. Truth changes your life, because truth isn't about opinions; truth is about reality.

Which leads me back to the importance of being devoted to seeking truth. Most people tell themselves stories about how good or bad, right or wrong, significant or insignificant their lives and problems are, and in some cases that I am aware of they would rather defend those stories to the grave than admit reality. When you are devoted to seeking truth you are defenceless; you don't have opinions and beliefs; you see everything for what it is or what it was. When you are devoted to seeking truth you surrender the fight to be right and you are prepared to give up your identity, in every sense, to reach that perspective.

Having said all that, being a devoted truth-seeker doesn't mean you are weak and you go along with the masses. In fact the opposite is true, because I actually believe it is impossible to know truth unless you have a deep sense of your own power and your own authority. Some people reading this may feel they already have that, but a quick look at the influential people in their lives and an assessment of their morals and values may reveal a different story. Having your own power and authority is about tapping into the truth that is inside of you, and that is an arduous journey that requires a depth of honesty and openness that is often beyond the bounds of reason and logic.

It is probably clear to see after reading this that people who are devoted to seeking truth are very rare individuals indeed, but it is also worth saying in conclusion that people who make it through to the other side and come to know truth have an inner flame inside them that is never extinguished and never flickers. They don't suffer with stress and anxiety or worry about past hurts and future problems, because the truth has set them free. The truth can do the same for you as well.

Questions for Reflection

- If I became devoted to seeking truth, what parts of my life would be affected?

- How much of my life is based on truth, and how much of my life is based on my opinions or the opinions of other people?

- Have I ever been silenced by truth? How can I apply that lesson to attract more truth into my life?

- What opinions about me, members of my family or my beliefs in general would I defend to the grave?

- How truthful are those opinions?

- To what extent do I have a sense of my own personal power and in what areas of my life do I seek out other people's opinions rather than my own truth?

Chapter 5
The Power of 'I Am'

'The ultimate truth of who you are is not I am this or I am that, but I am.' – Eckhart Tolle

As anyone who knows me will tell you, nothing I do or say is accidental. So now that you have reached the final chapter, I want to give you some information about why this book is based around the words 'I Am.'

The reason for using these words in the title and structure of this book is that they are believed to be incredibly powerful, as they relate to the 'G' word … yes, that's right, God – and in particular to God's name!

'I'm an Ignostic; I refuse to be drawn on the question of whether or not God exists until someone properly defines the terms.' – John Lloyd

Now, before I explain this controversial concept further, let me just define the difference, as I see it, between God and the dogma of religion. For me, religious dogma is about power-brokering, control and fear. It is man-made and is the cause of so much unrest and war. God is about truth, and truth is what you will find at the heart of every spiritual tradition.

> *'The truth is incontrovertible. Malice may attack it,*
> *ignorance may deride it, but in the end, there it is.'*
> – Winston Churchill

So with that in mind, let me share some words of truth
about God's name from the Bible. This excerpt is taken
from the third chapter of Exodus; incidentally, the reason
I believe these words to be truthful (or full of truth) is
because they cannot be used to control or manipulate.

> *Then Moses said to God, 'Behold, I am going to the*
> *sons of Israel, and I shall say to them, "The God of*
> *your fathers has sent me to you." Now they may say*
> *to me, "What is His name?" What shall I say to*
> *them?' And God said to Moses, 'I AM WHO I AM';*
> *and He said, 'Thus you shall say to the sons of Israel,*
> *"I AM has sent me to you."' And God, furthermore,*
> *said to Moses, 'Thus you shall say to the sons of*
> *Israel, "The Lord, the God of Abraham, the God of*
> *Isaac, and the God of Jacob, has sent me to you."*
> *This is My name forever, and this is My memorial-*
> *name to all generations.'*

So in this conversation between Moses and God, we learn
that 'I Am' is the name of God, and as a result many
people, myself included, believe that the moment we say
the words 'I Am', we set in motion an inherent power
within ourselves. Many people also believe that the underlying premise of this conversation also points to the
concept that 'I Am' resides in each and every one of us as
our own unique manifestation of the Divine.

Now there may be people reading this playing devil's advocate and thinking, 'How does this theory work in other languages?', 'It's all a bit too tenuous', or even 'What a load of rubbish.' To those people who can only think literally I say, no problem. Put this book down now and come back to it when you are ready. My aim is not to persuade you or convince you or argue with you about these thoughts. My aim is to give you clear information that has the potential to empower you forever.

You see, even if I didn't believe in a greater force, a higher truth bigger than myself, I would still be open-minded enough to realise that the words 'I Am' are enormously influential. This is because I have studied language patterns and communication structures my entire adult life, and I know that the right word, at the right time, said in the right way, with the right feeling attached, can make or break a conversation. There is no doubt in my mind, having studied the power of communication and the significance of the words 'I Am', that these three letters are life-changing.

> *'The words "I Am" are potent words; be careful what you hitch them to. The thing you're claiming has a way of reaching back and claiming you.'*
> – A L Kitselman

Think about how many times you use them in your daily life. How often do you identify yourself using the prefix 'I Am'? When you think about this you may be surprised at the level of unconsciousness you have about these words, but that is the point. I want you to become really focused on the words 'I Am' now. I want you to feel the words 'I Am' when you say them, and I want you to use the words 'I Am' with intention.

Do You Have to Believe in God for the 'I Am' to Work?

If you are asking this question, the chances are that you still haven't managed to divorce God from religious dogma. It may help you to think of God as the power we all have inside of ourselves to create and do good. I also think of God as all that was, all that is and all that ever will be. To me God is that greater force, that bigger truth. As the author Caroline Myss rather humorously says, 'I have no time for religion, to me religion is a costume party.' Having said that, I do have the utmost respect for all traditions and all faiths that teach truth, but I certainly have no time for any organisation that uses fear to control other people.

Is 'I Am' Just Another Affirmation?

Unless limiting beliefs stored in the subconscious have been addressed it is my experience that affirmations are not the most effective or efficient way of making transformational changes. This is because affirmations are very often used to affirm a belief consciously so that it is no longer contrary to the subconscious. For example, you may be aware of people with low self-esteem chanting 'I am rich,' 'I am happy' or 'I am beautiful' to improve their lives, and it would be fair to say that these types of affirmations can and do work for some people. However, I am suggesting that you harness the power of these words in a much deeper way by first understanding the *significance* of them and secondly by feeling them congruently in your body, mind and spirit at a conscious and subconscious level. We are able to use the words 'I Am' in this way when we begin to understand who we really are – something I hope this book is helping you to discover.

What Do You Mean, 'the Significance of the Words "I Am"?' This All Sounds Like God Again

Oh, my goodness [silent scream] – it never ceases to amaze me how powerfully people have been hypnotised to fear any thought about that three-letter word beginning with G! This disconnection with a greater force is, I believe, one of the biggest reasons why we are individually and collectively facing so many crises. Look, think of a gardener who sows a seed in the soil and nurtures that seed until such time as it has grown big enough to harvest and eat. That whole process makes total sense to us, but go deeper. No one can argue that a greater force was involved as well, because no amount of attention from the gardener could have replaced the part that a much greater force played in that process as well. The gardener didn't programme the sun to shine, the rain to fall or the growth of the seed to evolve; this part was taken care of by a force with much greater knowledge, wisdom and patience than us. Some people would call this force Nature, but again, go deeper. Just because we have given something a name doesn't mean we understand it.

The same miracle was experienced when you were conceived. You didn't consciously will yourself to grow a nose, a leg or even your own reproductive organs, which would later make it possible for you, potentially, to continue the miracle of life for further generations. The reasons why we or anything else exists in any way, shape or form are completely unreasonable if you spend a fraction of energy considering them at a deep level.

> 'That deep emotional conviction of the presence of a superior reasoning power, which is revealed in the incomprehensible universe, forms my idea of God.'
> – Albert Einstein

Yes, there is so much that science has been able to explain, but there is so much more that it hasn't been able to fathom. I am asking you to get in touch with that wonder, that mystery, that sense of awe again, because if you can, it will help you to heal and it will change your life.

> 'We don't know one-millionth of one percent about anything.'
> – Thomas Edison

So with humility in your heart about how little humanity actually knows, I hope now after reading this chapter you will put this information, together with everything else you have absorbed in this book, and consider harnessing the significance and the infinite power of the words 'I Am' as well.

'I am Master of my world

I am the Victorious Intelligence governing it

I send forth into this world this Mighty Radiant Intelligent Energy of God

I command it to create all Perfection – to draw to me the Opulence of God made visible in my hands to use

I am no longer the Babe but the Master grown to Full Stature and I speak and command with authority.'

– extract from *The I Am Discourses*

by Godfre Ray King

Afterword
'All is Forgiven'

'Sometimes letting things go is an act of far greater power than defending or hanging on.' – Eckhart Tolle

I have deliberately kept my personal stories to a minimum in this book. My aim was to include just enough information about myself to highlight how so much of this knowledge has come from my own experiences, without going overboard.

However, I do acknowledge that all good stories require a beginning, middle and end, so I wanted to close this book with a brief explanation of what happened when I said goodbye to my mother for the last time. I have chosen to focus on my mother throughout this book because she was more influential to me than my father, whom I may go into more detail about at another time. So because I have referenced my mother in the pages you have just read, it seems only right that I share what became of her and our relationship.

As you already know I was not close with my mother; she never expressed any kind of fondness towards me. I don't say that for sympathy, because I never knew any different, to me it was just the way it was. I say it because it was the reality, the truth. However, even though there was no love lost, I certainly knew that I belonged to her, because she would often remind me that she was the one who brought me into the world. 'I bore yee' she'd scream at me in a drunken drawl, usually when I refused to supply her with more alcohol (on more than one occasion).

Again, though, I do want to stress that I don't think of her as being good or bad, loving or unloving or any other extremes. Instead I always reflect on the reality of who my mother was. So, yes, I can remember her alcoholism and all the consequences of it, but I can also say with all honesty and integrity that if you met her when she was sober you would have liked her. She could draw people to her, she would talk to anyone and she would give away her last penny if you needed it. She also had incredible gifts. I have already mentioned her intuition, but she also played music on the piano and accordion by ear and she was also extremely adept at delivering wonderfully clever 'one liners', either as jokes or as a way of keeping people in check.

So I am grateful that, although I would have witnessed her demons during the first seven years of my life with her in Ireland, I would also have absorbed her true nature as well. Having said that I wasn't consciously aware back then of anything that I was being exposed to in any way, shape or form; it is only in deep reflection as I have got older that I have made these connections about the reality of who she was. I often wonder how different the world would be if we were all able to see the reality of our parents, rather than the good or bad, the right or the wrong.

Anyway, during my time at the orphanage I would visit her at weekends and holidays, but our relationship never developed. She brought me into the world and that was that. Even when I left the orphanage at age 15 I knew I had to support myself, and it was also at this age that I knew I had to sever all ties with her if I were to become a better person.

I remember the day I walked away from her behaviour so well. I had gone to her flat in London (she moved from Ireland at the same time as she placed me in the children's home) to make myself some lunch, and while I was eating she returned drunk again with yet another male friend. She staggered through the door and as I looked up I delivered a 'one liner' of my own: 'Don't tell me,' I said, 'Which Uncle is this?' As you can imagine she didn't take too kindly to my cheek, and told me so in language that I won't repeat, but when she had finished I stood up calmly and I said, 'I'm going now, and I'm not coming back.' And I never did. That was the last argument I had with her, and I knew there was no other option. If I had allowed myself to remain in her life I would never have started my own healing journey.

This wasn't the day I said goodbye to her for the last time, though; that happened when she was dying of bone cancer in hospital in 1979. The emotional upheavals that I am in no doubt she suffered and her love of drink had finally taken their toll and I got the call from a member of the family to say that she was literally on her death bed, so I went to see her.

I remember visiting her and being quite shocked at her physical condition. She was skin and bone and incredibly weak. This once stunning woman full of beauty and charm (despite the drink) was now just a skeleton who looked full of fear, regret and pain. There was even one occasion when I took myself off to another room to cry, not because she was dying but because she was suffering and I could see it, I could feel it. I also knew she was finding it difficult to die because as a Catholic she believed she would be punished for her sins, so to say she was absolutely petrified of meeting her maker is probably the understatement of the century. In fact the doctors told me several times that they couldn't understand how she was still alive, but I knew it was because she was too scared to die. I knew this so deeply that I asked her on several occasions if any thought (apart from her physical condition, of course) was bothering her. Each time she said no. The strength of her denial, even on the verge of death, was quite remarkable.

So at the end of one particular visit I stood up to go home (fully expecting to come back the next day and watch her continue her fight with death) and as I said goodbye she (quite remarkably for her) asked me not to leave. I was now almost 30 years old and I can assure you I had never heard her say anything like that to me before, but I had to go. I had built a life away from her and I was being called elsewhere. I also knew that *she* had to go, but at the same time I was very aware that there was something she desperately needed to hear. So without any conscious thought, I told her that 'all was forgiven.' Those words were expressed implicitly and explicitly, I didn't just say them. I felt them, I meant them, and because of her religious upbringing I believe she connected with the meaning of forgiveness at a very deep level. She died that night.

It is worth noting that the final conversation I had with my mum didn't instantly free me from all of the emotions I had to face in later life, but it did allow me to move forward so that I could find some really significant answers about who I really am, which is what this whole book is about: moving forward and finding answers about who *you* really are.

> *Moving forward and finding answers so that you can say with all conviction in your body, mind and spirit* ... 'I Am Healing'.

Further Reading and Resources

As I have mentioned throughout this book, I have produced various meditations to help you attune your subconscious mind and body to silence and stillness. I have also created recordings to assist you in the hugely important task of reconnecting with your physical body after experiencing trauma. For more information about these audios please visit www.thewysecentre.co.uk

Useful Links and Sources

Eckhart Tolle www.eckharttolle.com
Caroline Myss www.myss.com
Steven Porges www.stephenporges.com
Wayne Dyer www.drwaynedyer.com
Deepak Chopra www.deepakchopra.com
Robert Scaer www.traumasoma.com
Eric Pearl www.thereconnection.com
Gary Craig www.emofree.com
Peter Levine www.traumahealing.com

Further Reading

Wyse, Austin and Bailey, Dawn, *Without the Woo Woo*
King, Godfre Ray, *The I Am Discourses*

Index

Lightning Source UK Ltd.
Milton Keynes UK
UKHW02f0832100918
328635UK00012B/494/P